FASCISM

Also by Ian Dunt

Brexit: What the Hell Happens Now?

How to Be a Liberal: The Story of Freedom and the Fight for Its Survival

How Westminster Works . . . and Why It Doesn't

Also by Dorian Lynskey

33 Revolutions per Minute: A History of Protest Songs

The Ministry of Truth: A Biography of George Orwell's *Nineteen Eighty-Four*

Everything Must Go: The Stories We Tell about the End of the World

FASCISM

The Story of an Idea

IAN DUNT &
DORIAN LYNSKEY

WEIDENFELD & NICOLSON

First published in Great Britain in 2024 by Weidenfeld & Nicolson,
an imprint of The Orion Publishing Group Ltd
Carmelite House, 50 Victoria Embankment
London EC4Y 0DZ

An Hachette UK Company

1 3 5 7 9 10 8 6 4 2

A CIP catalogue record for this book is
available from the British Library.

ISBN (Mass Market Paperback) 978 1 3996 1292 0
ISBN (eBook) 978 1 3996 1293 7
ISBN (Audio) 978 1 3996 1294 4

Typeset by Input Data Services Ltd, Bridgwater, Somerset

Printed in Great Britain by Clays Ltd, Elcograf, S.p.A.

www.weidenfeldandnicolson.co.uk
www.orionbooks.co.uk

Contents

Of all the unanswered questions of our time, perhaps the most important is: 'What is Fascism?'

— George Orwell (1944)

INTRODUCTION
What Is Fascism?

The problem with writing about fascism is that no one can say precisely what it is. There are two versions of it in the popular imagination. The first is vivid and monstrous – a journey to the furthest possibilities of human evil. Adolf Hitler barking out violent fantasies from a podium. Benito Mussolini glaring at an adoring crowd. The murder factories. The uniformed thugs. The mechanisation of man.

The second is broad, shallow and ubiquitous. It's a cheap insult we throw around any time we come across someone with a whiff of the authoritarian: the overbearing politician, the dogmatic activist, the busybody, the ticket inspector.

The word fascism therefore leads a double life. It is serious and frivolous, existential and glib. And then, when you peer more closely, it threatens to disintegrate altogether. Scholars don't even agree on what fascism meant between 1922 and 1945, let alone what it might mean today. Arguments about who is and is not a fascist are now so mainstream they informed a joke in Greta Gerwig's billion-dollar 2023 block-buster *Barbie*. When Margot Robbie's Barbie ventures into the real world, a surly high-schooler calls her a fascist. 'She thinks I'm a fascist?' Barbie protests. 'I don't control the railways or the flow of commerce.'

Confusion is inevitable because fascism has no clear-cut intellectual basis. Most major political ideologies have a hefty theoretical grounding, based on the work of great thinkers. Conservatism has Edmund Burke, liberalism has John Stuart Mill, socialism has Karl Marx. But fascism is not a coherent ideology. Mussolini's 'The Doctrine of Fascism' was an extended encyclopedia entry published 13 years into fascism's lifespan, while Hitler's *Mein Kampf* was a deranged screed of personal grievances and prejudices. While Joseph Stalin agonised over proving, however dishonestly, that his actions conformed to Marxist and Leninist doctrine, fascist leaders did not bother justifying themselves at all, because there was no doctrine to follow.

Fascism, then, is more of an energy than an ideology. It does not communicate through the mind. It is pumped into the heart and enforced by the fist. It is intellectually vacuous and constantly shifting. When the term first appeared in Italy in 1919, fascism short-circuited conventional assumptions about the political spectrum. It combined the ancient and the modern, mysticism and bureaucracy, left and right, the mob and the machine, in unprecedented and sometimes inexplicable ways. 'Whichever way we approach fascism,' wrote the Spanish philosopher José Ortega y Gasset in 1927, 'we find that it is simultaneously one thing and the contrary, it is A and not A.'

Yet the paradoxes of fascism are a strength rather than a weakness. It weaponises its contradictions to maximise both its appeal and its freedom to act as it wishes. There is therefore no such thing as a pure version of fascism.

People have been arguing about the nature of fascism since at least 1922, when Mussolini became Italy's prime minister, and they are still arguing about it now. They use the word in two distinct but connected ways: the first is a description of a historical movement, and the second is a contemporary warning about what might happen next.

The historical approach presumes that fascism can only be understood in retrospect, based more on what fascist regimes did than what they said. But even this does not achieve total clarity. Each fascist party around the world behaved in strikingly different ways. The two most prominent and successful fascist movements, in Italy and Germany, had as much that divided them as united them.

Even within each country, fascism was a shapeshifter whose self-image did not align with its actual conduct. Fascist leaders wanted the world to see their societies as great coordinated machines working in perfect unity. But in reality, they were chaotic, messy compromises, riven by internal tensions and rivalries. Many of fascism's aims evolved according to whatever was most convenient at the time. It was fluid, opportunistic and contradictory.

The body of scholarly work on fascism is therefore incapable of consensus. The most prominent thinkers on the subject, including Robert O. Paxton, Roger Griffin, Zeev Sternhell and Stanley G. Payne, have been trying for decades to come up with a watertight definition, but every proposal has been either too narrow or too broad. Other writers have attempted to address fascism's inconsistencies and absences by compiling checklists of characteristics, but they are just as unsatisfactory. The *Oxford English Dictionary*'s definition is accurate but incomplete: 'An authoritarian and nationalistic system of government and social organisation which emerged after the end of the First World War in 1918, and became a prominent force in European politics during the 1920s and 1930s, most notably in Italy and Germany; (later also) an extreme right-wing political ideology based on the principles underlying this system.'

Another problem – for historians, though not the world – is that we didn't get to see how fascism might have evolved if it had not self-immolated in the furnace of war. Perhaps Hitler and Mussolini might have died in their beds decades later, like Spain's General Franco or Portugal's Antonio Salazar, their regimes having degraded into more conventional authoritarian dictatorships. Or perhaps fascism was inherently so unstable that it would have devoured itself in some other way.

Even during the lifetimes of Hitler and Mussolini, the word roamed wildly. In 1936, the anti-fascist American journalist Dorothy Thompson complained that the far left 'stupidly . . . label everybody who does not agree with them "Fascists"'. In his 1944 essay 'What Is Fascism?', George Orwell remarked that he had heard the word applied to not just political factions but 'farmers, shopkeepers, Social Credit, corporal punishment, fox-hunting, bull-fighting, the 1922 Committee, the 1941 Committee, Kipling, Gandhi, Chiang Kai-Shek, homosexuality, Priestley's broadcasts, Youth Hostels, astrology, women, dogs and I do not know what else'.

Fascism's incredible messiness allows for partisan mischief – bad-faith actors simplifying history to make points about present-day politics and assign all the blame to their enemies. Conservatives pounce with glee on fascism's debt to socialism, while leftists focus on the complicity of conservatives. Both camps are engaged in ignoring inconvenient facts. German and Italian fascists themselves claimed that they had transcended traditional notions of left and right.

The contemporary approach is to reduce the emphasis on historical details and instead treat the word fascism as a red alert – a clarion call to democrats that something especially malign and dangerous is taking place. It means we are less interested in explaining what happened in Europe a century ago than in identifying warning signs about what might take place in the future. The goal is to raise the alarm in the spirit of the old anti-fascist slogan: 'Never Again'.

This is often done sloppily, without any serious engagement with how fascism truly functioned. It can sometimes seem as if only the emotive label *fascist* can signal sufficient concern, as if calling a politician a 'far-right ethno-nationalist authoritarian' is somehow not taking them seriously enough. In the words of fascism expert Roger Griffin: 'You can be a total xenophobic racist male chauvinist bastard and still not be a fascist.' Sometimes this is done cynically, as an attempt to associate whichever group you don't like with the moral horror of fascism's worst crimes: Christofascism, Islamofascism, ecofascism, woke fascism, even liberal fascism. As a result, the word is typically more of an insult than a diagnosis. And each time it is used in this way, it loses some of its power.

These arguments became much more urgent and mainstream with Donald Trump's shocking ascendancy to the White House in 2016, which propelled him into an international brotherhood of authoritarians alongside the likes of Russia's Vladimir Putin and Hungary's Viktor Orbán. As the democratically elected candidate of one of America's two major parties, Trump was no 1930s-style fascist, but his rhetoric, policies and bullish contempt for democratic norms, culminating in his efforts to overturn the results of the 2020 election, nudged his administration closer to fascism than any in the country's history. President Joe Biden, not a man prone to hyperbole, later described Trump's Make America Great Again (MAGA) movement as 'semi-fascist'.

The specific circumstances that birthed fascism between the two world wars no longer exist, but the energy that drove it does. All around us, we can see an obsession with national rebirth, the demonisation of enemies, and the channelling of material anxieties into violent, irrational, conspiratorial, apocalyptic movements. It is that dark blood-magic that distinguishes fascism from conventional hard-right governments. As new books about fascism and the fragility of democracy filled the shelves during the Trump administration, some anxious readers revisited old ones such as Orwell's *Nineteen Eighty-Four* and *It Can't Happen Here*, Sinclair Lewis's 1935 novel about an American fascist takeover. While it is dangerous to meet complacency with hysteria, it is important to remember that something akin to fascism *can* always happen here. No country is inherently immune. No electorate is so sophisticated that it cannot become vulnerable to fascism's psychological temptations. As the Austrian psychologist Wilhelm Reich wrote in 1933: 'There is not a single individual who does not bear the elements of fascist feeling and thinking in his structure.'

This, then, is the moral lesson of the story of fascism. It is not necessarily about precise definitions, or watertight checklists, or strictly policed usage. It is about recognising that fascism appeals to some of the darkest instincts of human nature: the hatred of difference, the yearning for order, the sublimation of the individual to the group, the enchantment of violence. At heart, Orwell suggested, fascism meant 'something cruel, unscrupulous, arrogant, obscurantist . . . almost any English person would accept "bully" as a synonym for "Fascist"'.

The story of fascism shows us what happens when these instincts are given free rein and reach their ultimate expression.

It therefore serves as a reminder to treat with extreme vigilance any individual or group that seeks to encourage those ideas, and to dedicate oneself to stopping them.

The first step in that process is to understand where fascism came from. This book will tell its origin story. Rather than join the long, fruitless hunt for a perfect definition, we will explain what happened, how it happened and why. Only then will we try to understand what fascism means and what form it might take in the present day. The story begins in the strangest of ways, with a motley crew of nationalists, anarchists, socialists, artists, war veterans and cranks in Italy in 1919.

CHAPTER ONE
Mussolini's Road to Power

On 12 September 1919, a feverish middle-aged man in a bright red Fiat filled with flowers led around 2,000 Italian war veterans and nationalists into the Adriatic port of Fiume. Fifty-six-year-old Gabriele D'Annunzio was perhaps Italy's most compelling celebrity: a poet, playwright, journalist, womaniser, ultra-nationalist and master self-promoter who had been honoured for his courageous escapades during the First World War. He wanted to replace democracy with rule by an elite of exceptional individuals who happened to be just like himself.

Until recently part of the Austro-Hungarian Empire, Fiume had a large Italian population, but the post-war peacemakers had granted it instead to the new nation of Yugoslavia. D'Annunzio, outraged by Italy's 'mutilated victory', had a very simple solution: he would march in and take it. Fearing that he would mount a coup against Rome if it moved against him, the Italian government was petrified into inaction. D'Annunzio declared himself the de facto dictator, or *Duce*, of the 'Republic of Carnaro' and ruled for a full 15 months before he was finally removed by force.

D'Annunzio has been called the John the Baptist of fascism. With his right-hand man, Alceste De Ambris, he drafted a proto-fascist constitution, persecuted Fiume's Slav population and used combat-seasoned militias to suppress dissent. More importantly, he invented the aesthetic of fascism. A narcissist with a flair for drama, he pioneered the black-shirt uniforms, the rousing speeches from a balcony, the street parades, the rhythmic call-and-response chants, the soldiers' anthem 'Giovinezza' ('Youth') and the stiff-armed Roman salute that is now synonymous with fascism. It was the politics of the piazza, not parliament. He was essentially remixing the images and rituals of ancient Rome for post-war Italian nationalists.

Back in Italy, another ambitious nationalist was monitoring the occupation with a mixture of admiration, embarrassment and envy. Six months before D'Annunzio's march, 35-year-old newspaper editor Benito Mussolini had launched a new movement. It came to be called fascism. Like D'Annunzio, Mussolini wanted to restore the glory of the Roman Empire, with himself as its Caesar. But unlike D'Annunzio, he knew how to play the game of politics. The Duce of Fiume was a colourful eccentric who burned himself out because he had no strategy. Mussolini saw in the rubble of his failure the components of future success.

Benito Amilcare Andrea Mussolini was born in humble circumstances on 29 July 1883 just outside Predappio, a small town near Ravenna. 'The fact that I was born among the common people put the trump cards in my hand,' he later said. His mother, Rosa, was a Catholic schoolteacher. His father, Alessandro, was a blacksmith and local politician who had been arrested for his socialist activism. Alessandro's ideological muddle of socialism, anarchism, nationalism and authoritarianism was a powerful influence on his son, whom he named after three celebrated revolutionaries.

As a student, Mussolini was neither promising nor popular: a stubborn, misanthropic loner with a violent streak. During his first decade after graduating, he was often gloomy and aimless, drifting around Europe. He was a drinker, gambler and womaniser whose seductions by his own account included rape.

Mussolini earned a living as a reluctant schoolteacher, disliked by both pupils and parents. But he found his calling during a spell in Switzerland as a socialist journalist whose prose was punchy, direct and brutally entertaining. His beliefs, however, were erratic, to put it kindly. Sometimes he identified as an anarchist and sometimes as an 'authoritarian communist'. He carried a medallion bearing the face of Karl Marx. According to biographer Denis Mack Smith, 'he appeared to adopt opinions merely because they fitted some new attitude or would help his career', and would justify his U-turns 'as an example of an inner intuition that he came to consider as infallible'. Though he read widely, contemporaries thought of him as more of an actor than an intellectual: a shallow and unoriginal thinker with a weathervane personality.

Nonetheless, after settling in Italy for good in 1910, he steadily became one of the country's most renowned socialist writers and editors. He also honed his oratory at political meetings, learning exactly which buttons to push to drive the crowd into a mounting frenzy.

Mussolini had a direct line to Italy's anxieties. A relative latecomer to unification, industrialisation and urbanisation, the country at that time was desperate to become a great power. In 1910, the Italian Nationalist Association party brought together some of the future constituents of the fascist coalition, including big business and middle-class professionals, to pursue proto-fascist goals: the strengthening of national unity through authoritarianism and military expansionism. But Mussolini was not among them. Nor was he a revolutionary syndicalist like De Ambris – radical, anti-democratic trade unionists who believed that 'one big union' could bring down the capitalist system with a general strike. At this point he was still firmly a man of the left. In 1911, when the nationalists and many syndicalists supported Italy's imperialist war in Libya, Mussolini was jailed for his part in an anti-war riot. The Italian flag, he wrote, was 'a rag to be planted on a dunghill. There are only two fatherlands in the world: that of the exploited and that of the exploiters.'

After his release, Mussolini became the energetic editor of the Italian Socialist Party's newspaper *Avanti!*, almost tripling its circulation. 'My newspaper was a weapon, a banner, my very soul,' he later said. 'I once thought of it as my favourite child.' He ran unsuccessfully as a Socialist candidate for the Chamber of Deputies, Italy's parliament, and then successfully as a councillor in Milan. But Mussolini was no orthodox socialist. While he had read Marx, he was far more excited by writers with stranger and more visceral ideas.

Fascism was neither inevitable nor predictable, but it drew on ideas that had been circulating in the European mind for decades. The end of the nineteenth century was a period of immense upheaval in the fields of politics, sociology, psychology, technology and medical science. In each country, the middle classes in particular were convulsed by paranoia about the unruly urban masses, the fate of the nation and the destiny of the race.

One popular idea was degeneration: the notion that the moral and physical health of Europe was in terminal decline unless drastic measures were taken to control reproduction. The new pseudoscience of eugenics ('race hygiene' in Germany) encouraged 'pure' citizens to procreate while discouraging or prohibiting the 'impure'. There were many candidates for this biological enemy within: Jews, immigrants, homosexuals, socialists, the working-class masses. Eugenics, like nationalism and socialism, prioritised the health of the group over the rights of the individual.

While eugenicists fetishised biology and statistics, other writers were delving into the murk of the human subconscious. The Austrian neurologist Sigmund Freud was taking expeditions into the id. The French intellectual Gustave Le Bon was constructing an analysis of mob psychology. Whereas liberal democracy was founded on the Enlightenment values of liberty, reason and progress, these thinkers unearthed a vast resource of untapped power in the realm of emotion and myth. This pointed to a new kind of politics in which the essence of the nation could be found in the ancient ties of blood and soil rather than the ballot box. It was something you felt, not something you pondered.

Mussolini called Le Bon's 1895 book *The Crowd: A Study of the Popular Mind* 'a masterful work' and read it many times. By describing the crowd as dangerously volatile but controllable by the right person, Le Bon foresaw the art of twentieth-century dictatorship: 'The multitude is always ready to listen to the strong-willed man, who knows how to impose himself on it. Men gathered in a crowd lose all force of will, and turn instinctively to the person who possesses the quality they lack.' As Mussolini revealingly rephrased it: 'The crowd loves strong men. The crowd is like a woman.'

Mussolini was attracted to such fashionable thinking about the power of extraordinary individuals to seize the reins of history, in contrast to the contemptible compromises and half-measures of liberal democracy. He devoured Friedrich Nietzsche's philosophy about the superman and the will to power. In Switzerland, he attended lectures by the Italian economist and sociologist Vilfredo Pareto, who argued that democracy was an illusion and all that really mattered was which elite was in charge.

The retired engineer and amateur theorist Georges Sorel had been sketching out a vision of what a new elite might look like. Sorel felt that the nations of Europe had become sleepy and decadent and needed some shocking, soul-stirring, violent upheaval, based on the power of myth rather than logic. Unlike Marx, he thought that a revolution could just as easily be based on nationalism ('the people') rather than class consciousness. When revolutionary syndicalism failed, he moved towards nationalism; when Lenin's Bolshevik Russian Revolution succeeded in October 1917, he turned back to communism. What mattered was results. 'I owe most to Georges Sorel,' Mussolini said years later. 'This master of syndicalism by his rough theories of revolutionary tactics has contributed most to form the discipline, energy and power of the fascist cohorts.'

To call all of these thinkers proto-fascists would be unfair, but they all helped to mould Mussolini's belief in a vigorous revolutionary aristocracy, unconstrained by conventional ideology and justified in the use of physical force. The idea of fascism, then, was latent in European culture, but it needed an unprecedented crisis to activate it. That crisis came in the form of the First World War.

When the war broke out on 28 July 1914, Italy was bitterly divided over whether to join it. The pro-war movement was a disparate alliance of people with often mutually exclusive goals. Some hoped it would lead to a revolution; others believed a grand conflict would instead strengthen the young nation. The common factor was nationalism: Italy first.

For a few weeks Mussolini stuck to the Socialist Party's anti-war line and called intervention an 'unpardonable crime', but he soon resigned from *Avanti!* and launched his own, pro-intervention newspaper in Milan, *Il Popolo d'Italia* (The Italian People), leading to his expulsion from the party. His shocked comrades assumed he had been bribed into changing his mind. As it happens, Mussolini's newspaper did later accept secret funding from the British and French governments, but his U-turn was sincere. The war had accelerated his journey away from Marxism's emphasis on class conflict towards revolutionary nationalism: 'Class reveals itself as a collection of interests – but the nation is a history of sentiments, traditions, language, culture, and race.' He insisted that he carried the true flame of socialism – *national* socialism. 'You cannot get rid of me because I am, and always will be, a Socialist,' he taunted his former allies. 'You hate me because you still love me!'

Mussolini also co-founded with Alceste De Ambris a pressure group to promote intervention: the Fasci d'Azione Rivoluzionaria (Leagues of Revolutionary Action). The fasces is a tight bundle of rods, sometimes encasing an axe. It symbolised the power of magistrates in ancient Rome but came to represent unity during the French and American revolutions: one rod can be broken, a bundle cannot. To this day it appears uncontroversially in such contexts as the flag of Ecuador, the state seal of Colorado and the coat of arms of Vilnius, Lithuania. In Italy, *fascio* meant a league with revolutionary ambitions. At this stage, fascism was not yet an idea. It was still a half-cooked soup of instincts, symbols and personal calculations.

The bitter argument between pro- and anti-war forces in Italy overrode traditional politics. Some syndicalists aligned with Mussolini. So did the poet Filippo Marinetti, founder of the belligerent Futurist art movement, who described war as 'the world's only hygiene'. Anyone who opposed the war, socialist or otherwise, was branded a 'defeatist'. The two camps clashed in the streets. And for the first time, Mussolini enjoyed the thrilling taste of political violence.

Italy finally declared war on Austria-Hungary in May 1915. In September, Mussolini was conscripted and sent to the Isonzo front, where he impressed his superiors and was promoted to sergeant. But in February 1917, he was injured by a mortar explosion during a training exercise and returned to Milan to resume editing *Il Popolo d'Italia*.

The more extreme and certain his editorials, the more readers he attracted, even if he contradicted his equally extreme and certain previous editorials. 'It makes little dif-ference to him what the flag is, whether that of Fascism or socialism,' wrote one early biographer, 'so long as he is its standard-bearer.' For Mussolini, only those who had fought possessed the strength and integrity required to rule the country: an aristocracy of the trenches. What was needed, he wrote, was a man 'ruthless and energetic enough to make a clean sweep' and make Italy great again.

Fascism only succeeds when the status quo fails, and there was no greater failure than the previously unimaginable carnage of the First World War. Italy, despite being on the winning side, had been humiliated by the debacle of the Battle of Caporetto in autumn 1917 – a lasting symbol of the liberal government's ineptitude. Overall, the country had lost more than 600,000 men. It was unclear exactly what it had gained.

The chaotic, traumatised post-war world didn't just pose formidable short-term challenges for governments; it shattered the old order and the liberal belief in progress. The new symbols of the age were barbed wire, machine guns and the technology of slaughter. An orgy of national hatred and senseless killing had mutilated the minds of an entire generation, creating a widespread sense of resentment and loss.

The war had also introduced democratic nations to the experience of mass mobilisation, centralised economies, restricted liberties and modern propaganda, all of which fascism would later exploit. And it hastened the Russian Revolution, which became a model for ruthless insurrectionary violence. According to the historian Stanley G. Payne, it was the Bolshevik Lenin who 'initiated most of the new practices and institutions of fascist-type regimes'.

On top of all that, the war created a vast reserve of aimless veterans, hungry for purpose. Poems and films might give the impression that all soldiers were reluctant conscripts, sickened and scared, but the truth was that some of them had never felt more alive. The trenches spawned a new collective identity, distinct from mainstream society: a cult of virility, violence, comradeship and self-sacrifice, forged in the heat of battle.

The war machine had ground them up and spat them out. They felt betrayed by the machinations of the peacemakers and the weakness of their political leaders. Plagued by inflation and unemployment, they were primed for extremism of one kind or another. Revolutionary socialism was the obvious destination, but Mussolini was about to provide a potent alternative. 'When I came back from the war, like so many,

I hated politics and politicians,' wrote the army captain and fascist Italo Balbo. 'Better to deny everything, to destroy everything, so as to rebuild everything from scratch. . . Without Mussolini, three-quarters of the Italian youth which had returned from the trenches would have become Bolsheviks.' Members of the Arditi, a fearsome elite commando group in the Italian army, were especially attracted to leaders like Mussolini and D'Annunzio, who gave them an opportunity to transition to fighting domestic enemies. Some became Mussolini's private goon squad, stewarding his public appearances in their distinctive black shirts.

The word *fascismo* came a little later, but fascism was born on 23 March 1919. It did not look like the future. On a rainy Sunday morning in Milan, a few dozen people gathered in a hall overlooking the Piazza San Sepolcro to witness Mussolini launch a group with the 'hard, metallic name' Fasci Italiani di Combattimento (Italian Combat League). They were an overwhelmingly young ragbag of war veterans, pro-war leftists and intellectuals, united on one point: the need to 'declare war on socialism . . . because it has opposed nationalism'.

Occupying a previously unmapped political space – both revolutionary and traditionalist – fascism was confusing from the very start. Mussolini was a political entrepreneur who cobbled together a movement from disparate components and only gradually finessed it into a coherent programme. So when the fascists published their first platform in June 1919, co-written by Marinetti and De Ambris, it was merely Mussolini's opening offer to the Italian people. To paraphrase the old joke: these were Mussolini's principles, but if the Italian people did not like them, he had others.

Some of the fascists' initial policy priorities were strikingly progressive: women's suffrage, proportional representation, a national minimum wage, an eight-hour working day, a lower retirement age, and heavy taxes on capital. They vigorously opposed the cornerstones of conservatism: monarchy, church and empire. 'We are libertarians above all,' Mussolini wrote, as if he were talking about a completely different movement, 'loving liberty for everyone, even for our enemies.' It was all ultimately meaningless. As he later admitted: 'Fascism was not the nursling of a doctrine previously drafted at a desk; it was born of the need for action, and was action; it was not a party but, in the first two years, an anti-party and a movement . . . a series of pointers, forecasts, hints.'

At heart, what fascism became was both a substitute religion and a conspiracy theory, founded on an apocalyptic myth of a decisive battle between good and evil: the nation is tormented by a rolling crisis that democracy cannot resolve; the race is in decline, undermined by enemies within; the only solution is a dynamic strongman who can purify and unite the chosen people and eliminate their foes by any means necessary. Only then can the nation attain the greatness that it rightfully deserves and fulfil its destiny as one of the prime movers of history. Although fascism's first wave included some feminists, the movement applied heavily gendered language to politics: liberalism, humanitarianism and democracy were weak, impotent and effeminate, while fascism was virile, active and strong.

At first, Mussolini's aspirations to remake Italy seemed like a pipe dream. In the elections of November 1919, Nicola Bombacci's Socialists became the largest party, followed by the Catholic Italian People's Party. The fascists, running on a radical left-wing platform, won zero seats. Not one person voted for Mussolini in his birthplace of Predappio. With the movement's membership crumbling, a depressed Mussolini considered quitting politics, leaving Italy and writing novels instead. As bad as those novels would have been, we should all be sorry he did not do so. Triumphant socialists paraded a coffin through Milan as a mocking symbol of his political career.

They couldn't have been more wrong. Within three and a half years, Mussolini would go from total failure to a palace in Rome. And the key to that success would lie not in his policies, but in violence, and the fear of violence. Mussolini may have fancied himself as an intellectual, but fascists weren't fighting a battle of ideas. As one put it: 'The fist is the synthesis of our theory.'

The Italian novelist Ignazio Silone described fascism as 'a counter-revolution against a revolution that never took place'. During the years following the Russian Revolution, the middle and upper classes in many European countries were terrified of something similar happening on their doorstep. In Italy, 1919 and 1920 were known as the 'two red years', as strikes and occupations swept the country. In parts of the countryside, trade unions and socialists were effectively in charge. In the cities, the factories of companies as important as Fiat and Pirelli were seized by the workers. Shops were smashed and looted in 'cost-of-living riots'. The authorities were incapable of cracking down on arson, intimidation and street fighting. The Socialist Party became dominated by its revolutionary maximalist wing, which declared: 'Let us do as in Russia.'

The red years did not lead to revolution, but they did give the fascists a licence for violence. On 15 April 1919, a group of fascists clashed with socialists and anarchists in the centre of Milan, killing three of them. They then stormed the offices of Mussolini's former newspaper, *Avanti!*, and set fire to the building. Dozens of police officers and *carabinieri* stood by and did nothing. This was the first sortie of the *squadristi*, armed thugs who claimed to be restoring order to Italy while in fact sowing chaos – a contradiction we will see throughout the fascist story. Think of the *squadristi*, or Blackshirts, as a paramilitary criminal gang whose goal was to smash the machinery of democracy even as they professed to be defending it from the communists.

More than Mussolini, regional leaders known as *ras* (after Ethiopian chieftains) called the shots. The young men of the *squadristi* enjoyed posing for team photographs, brandishing cudgels and guns, before embarking on an 'action'. Clean-shaven or sporting neat moustaches, they appeared sleek and modern next to the bearded old guard. One of their signature tactics was to force victims to drink castor oil, a powerful laxative that one Blackshirt called 'the golden nectar of nausea'. Young men who had never engaged in politics before were thrilled by this new, aggressive anti-politics. 'Fascism has mobilized its forces from the twilight zone of political life,' observed the fascist Agostino Lanzillo, 'and from this derives the violence and juvenile exuberance of its conduct.' Their motto was *me ne frego*: 'I don't give a damn.'

The Blackshirts ran riot across the country, wrecking hundreds of socialist offices, clubs, newspapers, cooperatives and labour exchanges. Northern towns with a long and proud history of left-wing organising – Bari, Ravenna, Milan – fell under fascist control akin to a military occupation. In some regions, the *squadristi* became a shadow government. The left couldn't win. Any violence prosecuted by socialists or anarchists invited crushing reprisals, while socialists who renounced violence were nonetheless harassed, intimidated, assaulted and murdered. The Italian fascists were actually more lethal than the Nazis at an equivalently early stage: between 1919 and 1922, as many as 2,000 leftists and 600 fascists were killed in political violence.

Why didn't the Italian government do anything to stop the violence? Partly because many members of the army, police and church hated the left too. From the struggling, resentful middle classes to wealthy landowners in the agricultural northern regions, fear of socialism was fascism's most effective recruiting sergeant.

Much though Mussolini disdained *ras*-dominated provincial fascism as representing 'the private interests of the most sinister and contemptible classes in Italy', he could not ignore its success. He was forced to choose between his principles and his opportunities, which was no choice at all. So he quickly dropped the radical left-wing planks of the 1919 platform to appease his new allies. If landowners and businessmen were amenable to fascism, then tax rises had to go. If the church was a potential ally, then Mussolini – a lifelong atheist who had often described religion as a mental illness – would make peace with the Vatican. And if King Victor Emmanuel III might one day usher Mussolini into power, then why continue to denounce the monarchy? Mussolini began talking aggressively about seizing territory from the Slavs. Left-leaning fascists such as De Ambris protested, but they were soon forced out. To broaden popular support, Mussolini claimed that fascism could appeal to 'aristocrats and democrats, revolutionaries and reactionaries, proletarians and anti-proletarians, pacifists and anti-pacifists'. It would be whatever it needed to be. It was everything and it was nothing.

Nevertheless, he feared he was losing control of his own movement to the *squadristi*. After he was elected to the chamber in May 1921, as one of 35 fascist deputies, he claimed that violence was 'not a system, nor an aestheticism, far less a sport' but a 'brutal necessity'. He even signed a 'Pact of Pacification' with the socialists, promising to rein in the Blackshirts. This was his short-lived bid for political respectability. But the leading *ras* – Italo Balbo, Dino Grandi and Roberto Farinacci – denounced him as a traitor and plotted to replace him with D'Annunzio. Any repudiation of violence was a de facto restriction of their power. Flexible as ever, Mussolini dumped the Pact of Pacification to save himself, but made sure to limit the power of the *ras* by turning his loose movement into the National Fascist Party. 'It was necessary to transform a mob into a party,' he later explained. He became known as *Il Duce*.

In spring 1922, *squadristi* violence accelerated to the point where Italy felt ungovernable. The opposition was fatally disunited. The socialists splintered on both flanks, producing the Italian Communist Party on the left, co-founded by Nicola Bombacci and Antonio Gramsci, and the ironically named Unitary Socialist Party on the reformist side. Neither was able to form a united anti-fascist front with the Catholics, which was the only thing that might have actually stopped Mussolini. By late 1922, the Fascist Party had some quarter of a million members – up from less than a thousand three years earlier.

What did the fascists want? Power, first and foremost. On 24 October 1922, Mussolini told the Fascist Congress in Naples: 'Our program is simple: we want to rule Italy. They ask us for programs but there are already too many. It is not programs that are wanting for the salvation of Italy but men and will power.' The Liberal prime minister, Luigi Facta, a weak and unpopular caretaker leader, ignored warnings that the fascists were planning to march on Rome to remove him. But that was precisely what they did.

For Mussolini, Rome was much more than the seat of government – it was the ancient heart of Italian nationalism. 'Rome is our point of departure and reference; it is our symbol or, if you wish, our myth,' he declared. 'We dream of a Roman Italy that is wise and strong, disciplined and imperial. Much of what was the immortal spirit of Rome resurges in Fascism.' A plot was hatched to seize the capital.

Mussolini himself waited nervously in Milan in case it all went wrong and he needed to make a run for Switzerland. In his place were the 'Quadrumvirs' (a Roman term for four leaders): Cesare Maria De Vecchi and 26-year-old Italo Balbo were *ras*, party secretary Michele Bianchi organised Blackshirt raids, and General Emilio De Bono was a decorated war hero. They were all experts in violence.

On the morning of 28 October 1922, the Quadrumvirs led an army of Blackshirts into Rome to demand Facta's resignation and the appointment of a fascist government. Across the country, Blackshirts seized control of council buildings, police stations and telephone exchanges. But even at this stage, the fascists could have been stopped. Most of the 30,000 would-be marchers were in fact turned back at checkpoints around the city and didn't enter the capital until the crisis was over. The March on Rome wasn't ultimately a *coup d'état* – it was leverage. Pressure from the streets wouldn't have worked without the compliance of the elites.

Facta asked Victor Emmanuel III to impose martial law and clear the streets, but the king refused. With that one decision, he ensured the triumph of fascism. Instead of stamping it out, he threw open the gates and invited it in. When Facta and his entire government resigned in protest, the king summoned

Mussolini to Rome, appointing him the prime minister of a coalition government on 29 October. And so, at the age of 39, Benito Mussolini became the world's first fascist leader, appointed in full accordance with the Italian constitution.

As we shall see, fascism was tried in dozens of countries but only prevailed in two. For fascism to take off, several conditions had to be met. A nation gripped by political and economic crisis. A failing establishment. A radical left with sufficient momentum to make fascism look like the lesser of two evils but not enough to stop it. Vested interests that saw the fascists' anti-socialist violence as useful but ultimately controllable. A leader charismatic enough to embody the movement's grand promises of national renewal and shrewd enough to make tactical concessions.

All of these features brought Mussolini and Hitler to the doorstep of power. To cross the threshold, however, they needed two more advantages: a divided opposition, and conservative elites – including the head of state – cynical and hubristic enough to decide that it was safer to bring the fascists into government than to resist them. In *The Origins of Totalitarianism*, Hannah Arendt described fascism as a 'temporary alliance between the mob and the elite'. Mussolini presented himself to establishment figures as the solution to Italy's political deadlock, even though his own followers had contributed to the instability he promised to resolve. His offer was double-edged: the fascists would pacify the socialists, and Mussolini would pacify the fascists. Weary of chaos, the citizens of Rome greeted his appointment with 'a fever of delight'.

Perhaps the king feared that a crackdown would trigger a civil war and divide the military, which was riddled with fascist sympathisers. Perhaps he secretly approved of the fascists. Or perhaps he thought that they could be normalised and contained. But he should have read the signs. For his crucial meeting with the king, Mussolini wore a black shirt and a pistol on his hip. He was telling Victor Emmanuel exactly what kind of man his new prime minister was.

CHAPTER TWO
Hitler's Road to Power

Adolf Hitler learned two lessons from Mussolini's march on Rome.

The first was about historical destiny. Once the Blackshirts had moved from the streets to the corridors of power, it was clear to him that democracy's days were numbered. Fascism was a wave sweeping Europe. It would wash away parliamentary squabbling in Germany just as it had in Italy. 'The brown shirt would probably not have existed without the black shirt,' Hitler said many years later. 'The march on Rome, in 1922, was one of the turning points of history.'

The second lesson was about tactics. Mussolini demonstrated that power could be seized through an organised march on the capital. And so Hitler formulated his own copycat version, with a plan to arrest the government of the state of Bavaria, force them to join his paramilitary forces, and then march on Berlin.

Hitler's attempt began on 8 November 1923, when he slipped into a meeting in a beer hall just outside Munich. A crowd of around 3,000 people was listening to a speech by Gustav Ritter von Kahr, the general commissioner of the state of Bavaria. Kahr was flanked by General Otto Hermann von Lossow, the army commander, and Hans Ritter von Seisser, the chief of police. If they could all be taken prisoner, the Bavarian government would effectively be captured. Outside, Hitler's heavily armed Brownshirt paramilitaries encircled the building. He was joined in some capacity by several future pillars of the Nazi regime: Rudolf Hess, Heinrich Himmler, Ernst Röhm, Alfred Rosenberg and Hermann Göring.

At 8.45 p.m., as Kahr was still talking, Hitler smashed his beer glass on the floor and rushed the stage, surrounded by armed guards. There was uproar. He told one of his men to fire his pistol into the ceiling. At this stage he was half insane with nerves. 'He was sweating considerably,' the historian David King wrote. 'He looked crazy, drunk or both.' Hitler marched Kahr, Lossow and Seisser into a side room and made them an offer. He was going to become the head of a new Reich government – if they joined him now, they would secure prominent positions in the regime.

The Bavarians were hesitant. These were not good men. They were reactionary, authoritarian and prejudiced. But they had their own plans for taking over Germany and didn't want to play second fiddle to this gibbering maniac. So Hitler tried a different gambit. He walked back into the beer hall and made a speech. This time, he wasn't nervous. He convinced the crowd of something his Nazi Party colleagues had recognised years ago: he was one of the most effective public speakers of his generation.

Like Mussolini, Hitler used simple ideas, expressed in short sentences, to stir the emotions rather than work the mind. The language was not really of politics but of religion: the Christ figure, reconfigured into a secular archetype of suffering and resurrection. He told a story of Germany brought low by Judas but potentially redeemed by a pure leader who stood above the normal compromises of politics. He would begin quietly, falteringly even, forcing the audience to draw closer and listen intently, then gradually work himself up into a state of barely controlled mania, building towards a climax of fierce indignation and emotion, his face glimmering, the veins in his neck threatening to pop out his collar, his shouting accompanied by carefully rehearsed gestures.

And through it all shone his fanatical hatred of the Jews: the tyrant manipulators whose plots had undermined the nation and mutilated its destiny. All the complex social, economic, military and political issues impacting Germany could be amalgamated into a single enemy. And then it could be eradicated.

By the time Hitler finished his speech, the crowd had shifted from wariness to adulation, as so many had done before and so many more would do in future. He glanced over at Kahr and the others, then looked back at the crowd. 'Can I tell them that you stand behind them?' he asked. A roar of agreement. Kahr buckled and agreed to join the uprising.

Hitler was triumphant. He told the crowd he would 'fulfil the promise I made myself five years ago to the day, as a blind cripple in an army hospital: never to rest or relax until . . . a Germany of power and greatness, of freedom and majesty, has been resurrected'.

Everything was moving in his direction. Surely, he thought, the fascist revolution was on the brink of success.

The wellspring of the events that ultimately brought the Nazis to power lay in one simple psychological fact: most Germans did not believe they had lost the First World War. There had been no decisive defeat in battle. No Allied soldier had set foot on German soil. The Armistice of November 1918 was therefore expected to be an equitable peace agreement between two sides who had tired of fighting, rather than a bludgeoning humiliation inflicted on Germany by its opponents.

This confusion was ruthlessly exploited by key figures in the military. First Quartermaster General Erich Ludendorff and Chief of the General Staff Paul von Hindenburg, the two men who had led the war effort, told the public that the military had been brave, dutiful and principled and would have been victorious if not for a 'secret, planned, demagogic campaign' to undermine them at home.

This was the 'stab-in-the-back' myth. It would become the primary narrative German society told itself about the period it lived in. Whoever the alleged traitors were at various points – Jews, socialists, mainstream politicians – they were usually referred to as the November Criminals. 'For thirty years the army was my pride,' said Kaiser Wilhelm II, the last emperor of Germany. 'For it I lived, upon it I laboured, and now, after four and a half brilliant years of war with unprecedented victories, it was forced to collapse by the stab-in-the-back from the dagger of the revolutionist, at the very moment when peace was within reach.'

Psychologically, then, the German public never had to grapple with defeat. Instead, every material loss, every deprivation or extraction of territory, every political humiliation, every economic calamity was treated as a supreme injustice. Germany's military leaders passed all responsibility to the politicians back home, who had to undertake the thankless work of sorting out peace terms. The democratic German Weimar Republic of the inter-war years was therefore born with a stain of illegitimacy.

When the terms became clear, they proved deeply shocking. The Armistice eradicated Germany's military capacity amid a punishing Allied blockade that drove the German people into starvation. The Treaty of Versailles, signed in June 1919, removed a tenth of Germany's population and 13 per cent of its territory. Impossibly onerous financial reparations pulverised its economic capacity. The army was restricted to 100,000 men; tanks were banned, the navy was dismantled, and the air force abolished.

Weimar's three main moderate parties – the socialist reformist Social Democrats, the liberal German Democratic Party, and the Catholic Centre Party – took the brunt of the public dismay. Collectively they won 76.2 per cent of the vote in January 1919. By June 1920, that had fallen to 48 per cent. From this point onwards, defenders of the Republic were in a permanent minority in the Reichstag, outnumbered by extremist parties on left and right who demanded its overthrow.

Things went from bad to worse. In 1921, the government tried to print more money in order to meet its reparations bills, but this simply crashed the value of the currency. In 1918, a dollar had been worth eight German marks. By December 1922, it was 7,000 marks. A year later, 4,200,000,000,000 marks. This was beyond the realms of human experience. Even today, it remains the most severe example of hyperinflation in history. Money lost all meaning. You could sit down to drink a coffee and find the price had risen by the time the bill arrived. Workers would collect their wages in wheelbarrows and rush to make essential purchases before they became unaffordable. It was an unfathomable degree of financial pain.

A new national bogeyman emerged: the financier, the moneylender, the capitalist vulture who profited from the misery and impoverishment of the nation. That villainous image corresponded neatly with the antisemitic caricature of the Jew as a scheming manipulator who brought nation states to their knees through speculation and lending. Men like Ludendorff were happy to make this association, blaming Jewish people for all manner of evils: leading the Communist Party, agreeing to the Treaty of Versailles, setting up the Weimar Republic. In 1923, a wave of violence saw synagogues attacked and Jewish cemeteries desecrated. Antisemitic rhetoric embedded itself in the day-to-day political language of Germany's parliament, the Reichstag, and newspapers, conflating the 'November Criminals' with the 'Jewish–Bolshevik conspiracy'.

There was no peacetime in Germany, not really. Psychologically, the nation remained at war with enemies without and within. The language of battle was absorbed into political rhetoric. Opponents became enemies. Debate became conflict. Other parties were to be smashed or destroyed. Terror and physical aggression were valid methods of political change. Uniforms were ubiquitous. In the Reichstag, debates routinely dissolved into chaos and expressions of contempt. On the street, organised gangs of thugs engaged in violence and outright murder. Political parties, even ostensibly respectable ones, soon accommodated themselves to this vicious new reality. They took on paramilitary wings, designed to provide security at meetings, dazzle the public with processions, and assault rivals. The Nationalists had the Fighting Leagues. The Social Democrats, the world's largest left-wing party, had the Reichsbanner Black-Red-Gold. The Communists had the Red Front Fighters' League.

This was the social and political milieu when Hitler entered Germany's national life: brutalised, humiliated, impoverished, chaotic and violent. It fitted him like a glove.

*

Hitler was born in Braunau am Inn, Austria, on 20 April 1889. Like Mussolini, he was an aimless and unremarkable young man. Just another alienated mediocrity.

The defining moment of his youth came in 1907, when his application to the Viennese Academy of Fine Arts was rejected. People sometimes imagine a sliding-doors alternate reality in which he was accepted and thereafter devoted his energies to painting, but Hitler's art was never distinct from his politics. He specialised in loveless, turgid re-creations of Vienna's public buildings – expressions of his psychological need for order. He was attracted to power rather than beauty. Hitler scratched out a meagre living selling paintings and raised his spirits by watching the operas of Richard Wagner – great soaring expressions of pan-German unity and romanticised national glory.

Vienna at the turn of the twentieth century was one of the world's first truly multi-ethnic cities. It was a hotbed of modernism, from the sensual paintings of Gustav Klimt and Egon Schiele and the twelve-tone music system of Arnold Schoenberg to the psychoanalytical theories of Sigmund Freud. It was a beautiful, multifaceted social experiment. Naturally Hitler hated it. It was also home to many antisemites, including its conservative mayor, Karl Lueger. This part he liked. Through reading the antisemitic pamphlets that proliferated in the city, Hitler developed a vast conspiracist theory of Jewish influence: 'I had ceased to be a weak-kneed cosmopolitan and became an antisemite.' He absorbed the work of two giants of pre-war German antisemitism, Theodor Fritsch and Houston Stewart Chamberlain.

Hitler's anti-communism was as apocalyptic as his antisemitism. If Marxism prevailed, he later wrote, 'this planet will, as it did thousands of years ago, move through the ether devoid of men.' Yet he looked jealously at the mass demonstrations of Austria's Marxist parties, who seemed to have a strength and dynamism lacking among their reactionary counterparts. 'The psyche of the broad masses is accessible only to what is strong and uncompromising,' he later wrote about a Social Democrat rally. 'I also came to understand that physical intimidation has its significance for the mass as well as the individual.'

In 1913, Hitler moved to Munich, where he kept on doing drab little watercolour postcards of buildings, over and over again, much more comfortable in the ethnic uniformity of the German city. And then came the moment that would give his life direction. There is a photo of him in Munich on 2 August 1914, at the outbreak of the First World War, his eyes burning with enthusiasm and something like relief. From that moment on, his jungle of yearnings and hatreds would coalesce into an articulable political view.

He joined the Bavarian army three days later and was sent to the Western Front. Here, amid the mud and the barbed wire, he found what he would later call a 'release from the painful feelings of my youth'. He won two medals for bravery, one of which was on the recommendation of a Jewish officer, not that this taught him anything. A month before the Armistice, he was caught in a mustard gas attack and sent home to recover in a military hospital. It was there that he learned of the German defeat. He went to his dormitory and wept, before coming to the entirely predictable conclusion that the Jews had betrayed his country.

On 12 September 1919, Hitler was sent by the army to a meeting of the German Workers' Party (DAP). Established in January by a locksmith called Anton Drexler, it was attracting modest support. The army wanted to see if it was a potential threat, or whether it could be brought into its orbit. There were many men like Drexler in post-war Germany, and many groups like the DAP. It was just another shard of the ethno-nationalist *Völkisch* movement, which for more than 20 years had been calling for a racially pure pan-German Reich, rooted in blood and soil. Like all these groups, the DAP denounced Marxists and Jews (often synonymous) as alien to the *Volk*. Their heroes were Nietzsche and Wagner. That day in September, Hitler watched proceedings with interest and ended up speaking himself. Drexler was impressed. Under orders, Hitler signed up for membership.

At DAP meetings he deployed oratorical skills he had learned from those Social Democrat rallies in Vienna, grounding nearly all his rhetoric in his hysterical hatred for the Jews. Jewish politicians had undermined the war effort. Jewish merchants were pushing up prices during hyperinflation. Jews were dividing the Aryan master race of Germans against themselves, by acting as capitalist exploiters on the one hand and communist revolutionaries on the other.

He was clear from the very beginning what the solution would be. The Jews were 'to be exterminated', he said on 6 April 1920. In January 1923, he said: 'We know that if they come to power, our heads will roll in the sand; but we also know that when we get our hands on power: then God have mercy on you.'

Before long, he was the party's main draw, attracting large crowds to public meetings in beer halls. It is hard now to put yourself in the mind of someone who thought Hitler was charismatic. In the words of British comic-book writer Rob Williams, he looked like 'an over-mothered pervert waiter'. But his shrill, frenzied manner proved extremely compelling to thousands of alienated young men. Before long he was the party's main draw. Put in charge of propaganda, he added 'National Socialist' to its name. The NSDAP was commonly abbreviated to the Nazi Party. By March 1920, Hitler had left the army to become a full-time party activist.

On 29 July 1921, he took control, becoming party chairman, 'with dictatorial powers', and began to craft a fascist methodology. In late 1922, he adopted the title of *Führer* – the German equivalent of *Duce*. Like Mussolini, he nurtured a cult of personality and entrenched it with the same social paraphernalia: elaborate standards, military uniforms, and the stiff-armed salute, received by the leader in a bent acceptance gesture. New recruit Hermann Göring thought the party itself was just a gang of 'Bavarian beer-swillers and backpackers', but Hitler was a man he could believe in.

'Hitler is Germany's Mussolini,' proclaimed Hermann Esser, the Nazis' first head of propaganda, immediately after the March on Rome. The Fascist Party and the Nazi Party were woven from the same cloth. They were committed to the basic precepts of fascism: ceaseless violence and militarism; implacable opposition to communism, socialism and liberalism; a disdain for democratic institutions; and above all else, the notion of unifying the nation through subordination to the group identity. But Hitler's obsession with race was his own deadly innovation.

Hitler developed a Nazi iconography, starting with the flag. The swastika (*Hakenkreuz*, or hooked cross, in German) had been circulating widely since the early 1900s, from ethno-nationalist groups to the UK's Boy Scouts. Hitler embedded it in a flag of black, white and red: the colours of the old German empire. 'The red expressed the social thought underlying the movement,' he explained. 'The white the national thought. And the swastika signified the mission allotted to us – the struggle for the victory of Aryan mankind.'

As party chairman, he turned up the violence. Until then, Germany's most violent post-war militia had been the Freikorps, whose victims included the communists Rosa Luxemburg and Karl Liebknecht. But they had been suppressed after the failed Kapp Putsch in March 1920, and many members, including Heinrich Himmler, Reinhard Heydrich and Martin Bormann, had since migrated to the Nazis.

On 14 September 1921, Hitler marched into a meeting of the secessionist Bavarian League with a squad of young Nazis. They invaded the stage and chanted Hitler's name as they beat up the speaker, Otto Ballerstedt, and threw him off the platform. Soon, like the *squadristi*, Nazis were fighting bloody street battles with political opponents, armed with knuckledusters, truncheons, pistols and grenades.

Conservatives sometimes claim that national socialism was just another form of socialism, and that fascism can therefore be blamed on the left. Socialists usually respond by denying any connection whatsoever. It is a very tiresome game of blame-by-association. The truth is this: while Hitler's brand of fascism was far less influenced by left-wing ideas than Mussolini's, they did play a role in the early days.

National socialism had certain similarities with traditional socialism. In both movements, personal interests and opinions were subsumed into the group identity. In the case of socialism, this was class identity. In the case of German fascism, it was race identity.

The official Nazi Party programme of 1920, written mostly by Hitler and Drexler, was predominantly a litany of far-right proposals, but there were a few appeals to the labour movement, including the abolition of unearned income, the confiscation of war profits and the nationalisation of business trusts.

This left-wing element of Nazism became more pronounced under Gregor Strasser, a pharmacist from Landshut. He was a powerfully effective organiser, sent by Hitler to win over industrial areas in the north. He did so by articulating a more explicit socialist agenda, with support from the similarly minded Joseph Goebbels. In February 1926, the pair tried to convince Hitler to support a campaign to expropriate the German princes, who had managed to retain their extensive properties during the Weimar period. Tellingly, Hitler was mortified by the idea, saying it was an intolerable attack on private property. After a meeting with Hitler, Goebbels recanted, cut ties with Strasser and became the party's chief propagandist.

The left wing of the party was weak and easily sidelined during the 1920s. By 1930, Strasser's brother, Otto, was left carrying the torch until a showdown with Hitler saw him resign from the party. As the left departed, big business slowly began to warm to Hitler, seeing him as a possible mechanism to eradicate the communist threat.

This fuelled the conventional Marxist view, still common today, that Nazism was basically just an extreme mutation of capitalism – a hooligan front for business interests. The German socialist playwright Bertolt Brecht called it 'the nakedest, most shameless, most oppressive, and most treacherous form of capitalism'. But that was no more accurate than the conservative claim that it was a form of socialism. Fixated on the inevitability of historical progress and the primacy of economic factors, Marxists were incapable of grasping the reality of fascism. Nazism's deep commitment to racial destiny was at best ambivalent and at worst openly disdainful of the capitalist view of a consumerist society, in which supply and demand were the motivating forces guiding human behaviour. The Nazis were engaged in something much more profound: a battle for the racial soul.

In November 1923, when Hitler marched into that Munich beer hall, it seemed as if everything was in his favour. But it wasn't to be. The Bavarian politicians backtracked and informed the authorities, and the Beer Hall Putsch ended in an inglorious street battle with police, leaving fourteen marchers dead, alongside four policemen. Hitler received a five-year prison sentence, although he only served one. The Nazis and Brownshirts were banned. In the absence of its leader, the party splintered into squabbling factions.

In his cell, Hitler made a crucial decision. Revolution, he realised, would not work. Without the army and key state institutions on his side, he had been unable to secure power. He could not adopt Mussolini's strategy of bluffing his way into government with a show of force. Instead, he would need to deploy his talent for propaganda and public speaking towards winning mass support in elections. Paramilitary violence would still form the bedrock of Nazi activity, but it would be aimed at increasing the party's electoral success.

While in prison, Hitler wrote his memoir-cum-manifesto *Mein Kampf* (*My Struggle*), which laid out his extravagant hatred for Jews, communists, democracy and the 'weak'. He described national socialism as not just a party but an all-encompassing *Weltanschauung* (worldview), 'a totalitarian view of human existence'. The book's working title, *Four and a Half Years of Struggle Against Lies, Stupidity and Cowardice*, hinted at both the turgid reading experience and the way in which incarceration fuelled his tremendous self-pity. George Orwell later caused controversy by writing that Hitler's 'pathetic, dog-like face, the face of a man suffering under intolerable wrongs', reminded him of paintings of Christ on the cross. But Hitler's persecution complex was indeed key to his appeal. The more his enemies attacked him, the more righteous he appeared. Orwell went on: 'He is the martyr, the victim . . . the self-sacrificing hero who fights single-handed against impossible odds.'

Censorship, for example, backfired. Regional efforts to ban Hitler's speeches and shut down Nazi newspapers allowed him to play the free-speech martyr, as many on the far right do today. 'Why is Adolf Hitler not allowed to speak?' asked one Nazi poster. 'Because he is ruthless in uncovering the rulers of the German economy, the international bank Jews and their lackeys, the Democrats, Marxists, Jesuits, and Free Masons! Because he wants to free the workers from the domination of big money!'

Slowly but surely, Hitler developed a clear party structure. The Nazis' paramilitary wing was initially called the 'hall protection' group, then the Gymnastics and Sports Section, and then the *Sturmabteilung* (Storm Division), or SA. This thug enforcement unit was colloquially known as the Brownshirts. The *Schutzstaffel* (Protection Formation), or SS, was initially Hitler's personal bodyguard, but under the leadership of Heinrich Himmler, it morphed into an internal party police, gathering evidence on political opponents and fellow Nazis alike. Finally it evolved into the core elite of the new order: the embodiment of racial purity, discipline, unquestioning obedience and lawless violence.

Violence was several things at once for the Nazi Party. It was, for most of them, the only kind of politics they'd ever really known. They would not have recognised Carl von Clausewitz's mantra that 'war is politics by other means'. Instead, politics was war by other means. They were the trenchocracy, or the children of the trenchocracy.

Violence was also a symbol. It was an expression of one of fascism's chief proposals about the world – that might makes right, that strength is the supreme virtue. It was a confirmation of the return of national virility, an emphatic rejection of the weakness that defined Germany after the war.

More subtly, violence also served as a communications strategy. The architect of this ingenious approach was Goebbels. The red on the party's flag and posters was designed to attract communists and socialists to the party meetings, which would prompt angry protests when the true nature of the event became clear, and often result in a brawl. Those events were covered in the local press, thereby promoting the relevance of the Nazis. 'It was immaterial whether [the newspapers] laughed at us or reviled us, whether they depicted us as fools or as criminals,' Hitler wrote. 'The important point was that they took notice of us.'

Finally, violence was the creation of a self-answering narrative. Throughout the 1920s and early 1930s, one of Hitler's chief messages was that only he could provide the kind of order that could save people from the chaos and violence they saw on the streets. But that chaos and violence was, in substantial part, due to the actions he had himself organised and encouraged. In this way, Hitler's Brownshirts precisely emulated Mussolini's Blackshirts. The violence of the Nazi Party created the conditions they could then point to as the reason they needed to exist. As Hannah Arendt wrote: 'Being in the centre of the movement, the leader can act as though he were above it.'

The violence was encouraged through the use of a specific form of communication. Hitler and Goebbels would give orders couched in aggressive but vague rhetoric. The rank and file would understand what was being asked of them and enthusiastically go about it, whether it was attacking a socialist march or targeting Jews. This system provided a veneer of respectability that allowed the Nazis to secure conservative middle-class support and exempt Hitler from blame for what the Brownshirts did. 'In the interest of the party,' an internal Nazi document noted, 'it is also in many cases the custom of the person issuing the command – precisely in cases of illegal political demonstrations – not to say everything and just to hint at what he wants to achieve with the order.'

As Hitler's oratorical power increased during the 1920s, Nazi rallies grew, moving from beer halls to massive open-air events. He marvelled at the fact that his followers didn't just think the same but looked the same: 'Look at these laughing eyes, this fanatical enthusiasm and you will discover . . . how a hundred thousand men in a movement become a single type.' To many Germans, Hitler offered an end to the division and squabbling of rival parties and ideologies – a route back to an imaginary past of unity and glory. 'Finally a practical proposal for the renewal of the people,' a young clerk wrote after hearing a Hitler speech. 'Destroy the parties! Do away with the classes! True national community!'

But Hitler hardly ever traded in specific proposals. He was all about big, sweeping, dramatic gestures. He was operating at a sub-rational level, appealing to the basic human yearning for belonging and purpose. The Nazi Party became a leadership cult dominated by symbolic expressions of machine-like conformity, notably the salutation 'Heil Hitler!'

This thrusting, vigorous approach also defined the party's internal structure. Key personnel won their status through struggle rather than selection. As Max Amann, a high-ranking Nazi, told a local party activist: 'Herr Hitler takes the view today more than ever that the most effective fighter in the National Socialist movement is the man who pushes his way through on the basis of his achievements as a leader.' This ceaseless action and mobilisation later defined the Nazis' model of the state, and eventually its military machine.

Before long, the party was a smooth-running political operation, with a sophisticated propaganda engine, a vicious paramilitary wing, an internal party police to maintain discipline, and a cabal of loyalists, including Goebbels, Himmler, Göring and Hess.

Hitler needed just one more thing: a crisis.

The Wall Street Crash began on 24 October 1929, with an outbreak of panic-selling on the New York stock exchange, and juddered outwards across the globe like shock waves from a bomb.

When American banks started calling in their loans, German industrial production collapsed. Banks started to fail. The country sank into a deep depression. By 1932, one in three German workers was out of work. Unemployment eradicated millions of men's sense of self-worth, priming them for the Nazi message of strength and identity through race. Poverty and desperation led to social breakdown. And as Communist Party membership tripled in just three years, it triggered a fear of revolution. As it had been in Italy, this was a mirage, but one that enabled Hitler to present himself as Germany's only possible saviour.

The depression also helped bring down the Grand Coalition

government in the Reichstag, in which the Social Democrats had worked relatively effectively with the so-called bourgeois parties. The People's Party broke with the coalition over the Social Democrats' refusal to cut unemployment benefits and on 27 March 1930, the government tendered its resignation. No one knew it at the time, but this relatively minor disagreement marked the start of the Weimar Republic's death throes. From this point on, no government would rule with the support of a parliamentary majority. The Communists completely missed the coming danger. Their leader, Ernst Thälmann, dismissed Hitler as 'little more than a nuisance, whose irrational propaganda and boisterous street marches should not be allowed to distract from the real battle against the Social Democrats'.

What followed was three years of elections, which hit Germany once every few months, like machine-gun fire. 'We come as enemies,' Goebbels boasted of the Nazis' parliamentary strategy. 'As the wolf descends on the flock, so do we come.' The Nazis would use democracy to destroy democracy.

The Reichstag elections of September 1930 put the Weimar system on life support. The Nazis went from securing 800,000 votes and 12 seats in 1928 to 6.4 million votes and 107 seats. Across the chamber, the Communist Party surged from 54 seats to 77. With the two chief enemies of the Republic now dominating the Reichstag, it became unmanageable. Eventually, it simply stopped bothering. Between July 1932 and February 1933, it convened for just three days. Power drained away from it. But power has to go somewhere. So it coalesced around President Paul von Hindenburg's inner circle, which planned to turn Germany into a conservative dictatorship.

Hindenburg chose as his chancellor the inept and morally vacuous aristocrat Franz von Papen, who wanted to roll back not just the Weimar Republic, but all European progress since the French Revolution. His most fateful decision was a strategic one. He decided to try and win over the Nazis to the cause, thereby allowing him to absorb into the dictatorship the kind of popular appeal he was unable to secure by himself. This is perhaps the most crucial moment in the story of how fascism took power in Germany.

It is an uncomfortable fact that no one is better at killing fascists than authoritarian conservatives. As we'll see, countries like Spain and Portugal were saved from the fascists by the defensive manoeuvres of dictators who were not ultimately that different from them but feared their volatility. In Germany, as in Italy, that did not happen. Instead, authoritarian conservatives decided to placate the fascists.

This does not mean that they were politically identical. The conservatives wanted to impose a traditional dictatorship. If someone was a political campaigner against the regime, they would have been imprisoned and probably killed. But as long as they did what they were told, kept their mouth shut, and did not complain about the removal of their rights, they would by and large have been left alone. The traditional institutions of the church and marriage would have been respected. It would have represented a return to the past, rather than a journey towards a new type of future.

Fascists, however, wanted access to people's souls. No part of private life would be spared their attention. No institution, no matter how old, would be respected. Society was to be moulded into a vast homogenous mass, enraptured in worship of race leadership. They were seeking the creation of a New Man for a new future: the total uniformity of the human spirit.

As an olive branch to Hitler, Papen called fresh elections for July 1932 and lifted a ban on the Brownshirts, leading to a predictable wave of street violence. By this stage, fascist methodology had corroded the behaviour of all the major parties. Even the earnest, law-abiding Social Democrats, the last defenders of the democratic Republic, were questioning the value of rationality in political discourse. The party hired the psychologist Sergei Chakhotin to advise them and concluded: 'We have to work on feelings, souls and emotions so that reason wins the victory.' They adopted a clenched-fist salute in response to the Nazi salute. The symbolic pharmacopoeia of fascism – its flags, gestures, marches, uniforms and slogans – had permeated the entire political culture.

Election posters were dominated by images of violence and destruction, no matter which party they represented. Germany had once symbolised itself through the gentle cartoon figure of German Michel – a dopey man in a gown and nightcap who looked like he'd just been startled out of a deep sleep. His self-mocking quality was similar to the stout, good-humoured image of Britain's John Bull. Now he was gone. This was not the time for mild self-effacement. He was replaced by the giant, athletic, half-naked Aryan man who came to represent Germany for all the parties. Posters would feature him destroying high finance for the Nazis, elbowing aside Nazis for the Social Democrats, or removing Communists for the Centre Party. Every image and symbol communicated the same message: the time for parliamentary debate and civil political disagreement was over. Now was the time for force. And for will.

For the Nazis, the July election result was a paper victory.

Although the party had doubled its vote to become the largest in the Reichstag, it had hit its electoral ceiling. Another election in November saw them running on empty. They'd used up all their funds, and their once magnetising campaign techniques had begun to seem like old hat. Hitler spoke to half-empty meeting halls. For the first time since the Great Depression hit, the Nazis' support fell. One newspaper called the Führer 'a failing comet in the November fog'.

Most alarmingly for Hitler, the economic situation was showing signs of improvement. Papen's successor, Kurt von Schleicher, initiated a massive job creation programme to relieve unemployment through public works – a kind of early German New Deal. Some prominent Nazis were getting restive. Hitler had to purge around 500 insubordinate Brownshirts and oust Gregor Strasser, the leading anti-capitalist Nazi, for negotiating with Schleicher behind his back. At this moment of weakness, his ambitions might have turned to ash.

But that did not happen. And the reason it did not happen was because conservative authoritarians did not want it to happen. Hindenburg and Papen thought the existing circumstances were perfect for their needs. If things improved too much, democracy could return, and the old Weimar parties might recover their influence. Germany's leaders had a choice. And they chose fascism.

On 30 January 1933, Hindenburg and Papen decided to offer Hitler the position of Reich chancellor. 'It is my unpleasant duty to appoint this fellow Hitler as chancellor,' Hindenburg confided. Hitler was sworn in at around 11.30 in the morning.

Just as the king of Italy thought he had clipped Mussolini's wings by making him a coalition prime minister, the older men thought they had controlled Hitler. The pair arranged the cabinet so that he was hemmed in on all sides by conservatives and received only two major offices of state: the chancellorship and ministry of the interior, held by Wilhelm Frick. Papen became vice chancellor and retained his close relationship with Hindenburg. 'Within two months,' he said, 'we will have pushed Hitler so far into a corner that he'll squeak.' The *New York Times* was similarly fooled: 'Hitler Puts Aside Aim to Be Dictator'. The paper assured readers that he had retreated from his demand to be 'the Mussolini of Germany'.

In reality, the arrangement provided the Nazis with everything they needed to secure total control of the country. They commanded not just the chancellorship but the domestic law-and-order apparatus. This would allow them to unleash Brownshirt violence across Germany, backed by the full force of the state.

Hindenburg and Papen 'have believed themselves to be very ingenious,' remarked the French ambassador André François-Poncet, 'ridding themselves of the wolf by introducing him into the sheepfold.' But the wolf had other plans.

CHAPTER THREE
Fascism in Power

Fascist Italy was up and running for a full decade before Nazi Germany, but today it inspires a puny fraction of the popular fascination and moral horror evoked by Hitlerism. While Hitler remains a symbol of almost supernatural evil, Mussolini is easily caricatured as a conceited buffoon. The historian A. J. P. Taylor dismissed his regime as a sham from start to finish: 'The social peril from which it saved Italy was a fraud; the revolution by which it seized power was a fraud; the ability and policy of Mussolini were fraudulent. Fascist rule was corrupt, incompetent, empty; Mussolini himself a vain, blundering boaster without either ideas or aims.'

This is a shabby legacy for the man who not only invented fascism but became its first world leader in the space of four years. And it would have stunned his contemporaries, who regarded him for a long time as one of the great statesmen of his era. From the moment he took office, Mussolini was an object of fascination. During his international debut at the Lausanne Conference in November 1922, one journalist observed: 'The fact was, nobody was interested in anyone but Mussolini.' In August 1923, he made the first of eight appearances on the cover of *Time* magazine. 'Fascismo has had a great deal of courage, very considerable wisdom, and immense luck,' declared *The Times* of London on the first anniversary of the March on Rome. 'On the whole, it has deserved the sincere birthday greetings of the world.'

Most foreign governments considered Italy an ungovernable basket case and were intrigued to see how its new leader fared, lauding him as a warrior for anti-socialism. Winston Churchill, then Britain's Chancellor of the Exchequer, visited Rome in 1927 and told a press conference: 'If I were Italian, I am sure I would have been with you from beginning to end in your struggle against the bestial appetites of Leninism.' This would later prove embarrassing for Churchill, but many other luminaries were similarly glowing. Mussolini's admirers, to varying degrees, included Sigmund Freud, the Indian nationalist Mahatma Gandhi, the writer G. K. Chesterton, the British war hero General Douglas Haig and the American inventor Thomas Edison, who called him 'the greatest genius of the modern age'. Mussolini was even favourably mentioned in P. G. Wodehouse's English rewrite of Cole Porter's 1934 hit 'You're the Top'. A dazzled *New York Times* reporter wrote from Rome: 'No other living man has become a historical figure as quickly as Mussolini . . . One may object to any form of dictatorship, but one cannot help being stimulated by the phenomenal vitality of this man.'

How did Mussolini seduce the world? For his first two years in office, he was frustrated, with only 32 Fascist deputies in a chamber of 535, and just 4 Fascist ministers in a cabinet of liberals, nationalists and Catholics. His first finance minister, Alberto de' Stefani, was an establishment centrist who privatised industries and cut taxes and spending. Mussolini struggled to reconcile the competing demands of his more conservative coalition partners, the voters who longed for stability, and the restless, hardline *squadristi*. 'Everywhere the

Fascist Party appears to be marked by divisions and personal quarrels,' he grumbled.

He had to play a delicate game, posing as the only man who could keep the Blackshirts on a leash and using the threat of them running wild to secure parliamentary approval for temporary emergency powers. He bragged to the chamber that he could 'easily have turned this dull and grey hall into a bivouac for my platoons' and issued an amnesty for anyone convicted of committing political violence, as long as it was 'for nationalist reasons'.

Behind the scenes, though, he had lost patience with the violence of provincial fascism. To enforce party discipline, he established an alternative cabinet called the Grand Council of Fascism, incorporated the Fasci Italiani di Combattimento into the armed forces, and legitimised the *squadristi* in the form of a new state militia under Emilio De Bono, known as the MVSN.

Acting as his own foreign minister, Mussolini flexed his muscles on the world stage by reclaiming the symbolic trophy of Fiume from Yugoslavia and defying the League of Nations with his brief occupation of the Greek island of Corfu. He also became the first Western leader to officially recognise the Soviet Union, leading to a surprisingly friendly relationship with Stalin, whom he approvingly – and not entirely wrongly – considered a 'cryptofascist'.

At home, he schemed and bullied his way towards greater power. The general election of April 1924 was the first and only ballot held under the new Acerbo Law, which gave the largest vote-winner a full two thirds of seats in the Chamber of Deputies. The National List – fascists plus conservatives – won by a landslide: 65 per cent of the vote and 374 of the chamber's 535 seats. But as a direct result of that election,

Mussolini faced a months-long crisis that almost finished him off.

On 30 May, Giacomo Matteotti, the moderate leader of the Unitary Socialist Party, stood up in parliament to accuse the fascists of intimidation and vote-rigging. Having already been kidnapped and tortured by fascists, he knew full well that this could be his suicide note. Eleven days later, he was snatched off the streets of central Rome in broad daylight and bundled into a Lancia. Five suspects were promptly arrested, including Cesare Rossi, Mussolini's chief press officer.

Although there is no solid evidence that Mussolini personally ordered the kidnapping, he took the flak. National outrage fuelled demonstrations calling for a general strike to bring down the government. The opposition parties tried various measures to force its collapse. Again the king could have removed Mussolini. Again he declined.

Still, the scandal rolled on throughout the summer, with the haggard, unshaven Mussolini vomiting blood from a stress-induced stomach ulcer. In August, Matteotti's corpse was discovered in a shallow grave in woods 20 kilometres from Rome. He had most likely been stabbed to death while trying to escape his abductors. Things finally came to a head on the last day of 1924, when the leading Blackshirts issued Mussolini an ultimatum: either crush the opposition or stand aside and let them do it. Far from backing down, they wanted to discharge the full force of fascist violence against their opponents.

Mussolini's judgement was often dreadful, but he was always at his most politically adept when he was on the ropes. In an ingeniously constructed speech on 3 January 1925, he took personal responsibility for any violence committed in the name of fascism: 'If fascism was just castor oil and cudgels and not a superb passion shared by the best of Italian youth, it is my fault.' But he denied ordering Matteotti's murder, and insisted that only he could guarantee peace and stability, 'with love, if possible, or with force, if necessary'. That speech marked the death of Italian democracy for the next 20 years, and the birth of Mussolini the dictator.

Under fascism, the leader represented the state and the state represented the pure will of the people. Therefore to oppose Mussolini was to oppose Italy itself. A slew of assassination attempts in 1925 and 1926, which collectively did nothing worse than graze his nose, burnished the idea that he was both threatened by enemies within and protected by God. They also justified an avalanche of repressive legislation.

As of Christmas Eve 1925, Mussolini was no longer the prime minister but Il Capo del Governo e Duce del Fascismo. Nor was he answerable to parliament; he could only be removed by the king. Elected mayors were replaced by fascist appointees called *podestà* and troublesome judges were removed. The fascists then made official dissent impossible by abolishing all other parties. For the elections of 1929 and 1934, voters could only vote for or against a list of candidates prepared by the Grand Council of Fascism. It won these referenda by 98.43 per cent and 99.85 per cent respectively. After that, elections ceased altogether.

Critical journalism was silenced by a combination of censorship laws and intimidation. A new secret police force, the Organization for Vigilance and Repression of Anti-Fascism (OVRA), became the model for Germany's Gestapo. As its agents compiled detailed files on around 130,000 alleged subversives, with the help of as many as 100,000 informants, Italy became a surveillance state.

Mussolini also whipped his own party into line. The *ras* had already tried to remove him twice, in 1921 and 1924. So he found ways to keep them busy. He gave Balbo responsibility for the air force and made Farinacci secretary of the Fascist Party. He removed some potential challengers from Italy altogether by making one former Quadrumvir, De Vecchi, the governor of Italian Somaliland and another, De Bono, the governor of Tripolitania in Libya. Barely a decade after going to jail for opposing the colonisation of Libya, Mussolini now saw the crushing of resistance forces as an essential first step towards his Roman dream of an Italian empire and great-power status.

The 'pacification' of Libya, which lasted from 1923 to 1934, would nowadays qualify as genocide. It escalated to mustard gas, massacres, executions and mass deportations. The entire Libyan population of Cyrenaica, the country's eastern region, was forcibly removed and crammed into concentration camps, ravaged by starvation and disease. 'The path has been set,' wrote one army officer in 1930, 'and we must follow it to the end, even if it entails the death of the entire population.' By the time Balbo, the new governor general, announced the creation of Italian Libya in 1934, an estimated 80,000 Libyans had died. The worst fascist violence committed by Mussolini's regime did not take place at home, but was exported to Africa.

The situationist Guy Debord described fascism as 'a cult of the archaic completely fitted out by modern technology'. It was a strange combination of the very old and the very new. On a practical level, it was an ultra-modern machine for exercising power, fit for the age of the aeroplane and the moving picture. But it drew its emotional power from an apocalyptic myth of national renewal. Fascism proposed that a once-mighty nation had grown weak, decadent and polluted. Only a project of violent cleansing could regenerate its soul and breed a New Man: virile, dynamic, patriotic, warrior-like. Mussolini summed it up in a 1926 speech: 'It is Fascism which has refashioned the character of the Italians, removing impurity from our souls, tempering us to all sacrifices, restoring the true aspect of strength and beauty to our Italian face.'

Having invented fascism, Mussolini also pioneered totalitarianism. The word *totalitario* began as an insult flung by the anti-fascist politician Giovanni Amendola, but it was deftly commandeered by Giovanni Gentile, Mussolini's favourite philosopher, to describe a society in which citizens conformed to the ideology of the state in every area of life. Mussolini later summed up totalitarianism more pithily: 'Everything within the state, nothing outside the state, nothing against the state.'

The fascists created a black mirror of existing institutions, from trade unions to youth groups, in order to extend the tendrils of fascism into every corner of Italian life. The Opera Nazionale Dopolavoro (National Afterwork Club) promoted sport, the arts and other leisure activities. But its enormous popularity was deceptive – most members enjoyed the diversions without associating them with fascism. Unlike Hitler or Stalin, Mussolini was never really able to drill his ideology into his citizens' brains. Italian fascism had far more passive accomplices than true believers. The bulk of its support came from the silent majority of Italians, who welcomed stability and could tolerate fascist repression as long as it didn't directly affect them.

Mussolini also failed to eliminate rival power bases. His 1929 Lateran Accords with the Vatican enabled the church to remain strong in the community. He never challenged the king, who retained his power to appoint and sack prime ministers. Nor did he threaten the conservative elites who had been his essential enablers. The party may have run the state, but it did not replace it in the same way that the Nazi Party consumed the German state. According to biographer Nicholas Farrell: 'The Italians never gave their consent to Fascism; they gave it to Mussolini.'

And who exactly was Mussolini? Despite his personal magnetism and indomitable public image, he was far from being the fascist New Man. In spring 1932, the German journalist Emil Ludwig pinned him down for a revealing series of interviews about his life and politics. Ludwig found himself 'dealing with a lion, mighty but high-strung and nervous', who spoke in a clipped, 'metallic' voice. 'I have no friends,' Mussolini told Ludwig. 'First of all, because of my temperament; secondly because of my view of human beings . . . Fundamentally I have always been alone.' He had several mistresses and thousands of lovers but no confidants and spent little time with his wife and children. He worked fanatically hard and lived frugally, giving away most of his income. He disliked travelling, socialising, Sundays and jokes. He was a meticulously neat hypochondriac who quit smoking and rarely touched alcohol, coffee or meat but still suffered from chronic anxiety-related stomach problems. He was also a superstitious man who believed in astrology, palm-reading and ghosts. This was a strange brew for a fascist superman.

Nonetheless, Mussolini keenly understood the job of a dictator: 'It is faith that moves mountains, not reason . . . Everything turns upon one's ability to control the masses like an artist.' To the public, Il Duce was a paradoxical combination of tribune of the common man and demigod, as he constructed a cult of personality that would be emulated by

Hitler and Stalin. Mussolini the actor took to the role with gusto. He had long since removed his glasses for photographs. Now he shaved his head to conceal his receding hairline and began posing with his shirt off. His block of a head and giant, jutting jaw, like an Easter Island statue, were everywhere. He was described as 'the world's most photographed man'.

'You could say that I spent the first twenty years of my life with Mussolini's face always in view,' recalled the writer Italo Calvino, who was born in 1923, 'in the sense that his portrait hung in every classroom as well as in every public building or office I entered.' Calvino summed up the radical new image of leadership that Il Duce sold to the Italian people: 'Energy, arrogance, bellicosity, the posture of a Roman *condottiero*, a plebeian pride that contrasted with everything that had until then formed the image of a statesman.'

Mussolini was a punchy phrasemaker: walls were stencilled with slogans such as 'Believe, Obey, Fight'. Followers took pilgrimages to his birthplace in Predappio. He even laid claim to one twenty-sixth of the alphabet: the letter M on public display could mean only one thing. 'When one speaks of fascism, one speaks of Him,' proclaimed a book for school-children. 'Fascism is his cause; he has created it, he has infused it with his spirit and given it life.' His popularity could not be attributed solely to bullying or brainwashing. He received up to 1,500 fan letters a day, many of them from women besotted with him. His sexual charisma, though hard to comprehend now, was real.

In October 1932, the fascists held nationwide celebrations of the tenth anniversary of the March on Rome, retrospectively turning it into a glorious revolution rather than a convergence of thuggery, elite compliance and good luck. The history of the three years preceding it had also been rewritten. Beaten and broken, the socialists suffered the final insult of being portrayed as the real aggressors from whom Italy needed to be saved. Soon, all Mussolini's prominent opponents would be either dead, incarcerated, missing or living in exile.

At last, 13 years after he invented fascism, Mussolini codified his ad hoc ideology in 'The Doctrine of Fascism', an essay co-written with Giovanni Gentile in 1927 but not published until 1932. The authors presented fascism as much more than a political movement. It was a new religion: 'Fascism, in short, is not only a law-giver and a founder of institutions, but an educator and a promoter of spiritual life.' But it was a spirituality based on perpetual struggle and submission to the state: 'Never before have the peoples thirsted for authority, direction, and order, as they do now. If every age has its doctrine, then innumerable symptoms indicate that the doctrine of our age is the Fascist.'

By the time Hitler took power, then, Mussolini had established the core tenets of fascism, but he did not believe that his Italian invention was easily exportable. 'I should be pleased I suppose that Hitler has carried out a revolution on our lines,' he said. 'But they are Germans. So they will end by ruining our idea.'

At around 9 p.m. on 27 February 1933, a young Dutchman called Marinus van der Lubbe slipped into the Reichstag parliament building in Berlin. His initial plan was to start a fire in the restaurant area by setting light to the furniture, but when that didn't work, he moved to the debating chamber itself, which proved highly combustible. Not long after he had entered, the whole building was ablaze.

Hitler rushed there as soon as he heard the news, flanked by Goebbels and Göring. 'Hitler had propped himself up on the stone parapet of the balcony with both arms and stared silently into the red sea of flames,' recalled Rudolf Diels, head of the Prussian political police. Hitler's face was 'flaming red with excitement' and his voice more hysterical than ever. 'There will be no more mercy now,' the Führer shrieked. 'Anyone who stands in our way will be butchered.'

Hitler blamed a communist conspiracy. The communists countered with claims of a Nazi conspiracy, with van der Lubbe the hapless scapegoat. The most reliable evidence supports the simplest version of events, which is that van der Lubbe was working alone, as he repeatedly insisted. The consequences, at least, are beyond debate. Hitler had been gifted the excuse to convert his chancellorship into despotism on an unforeseen scale.

This time, the wave of violence would not be carried out by Brownshirts acting alone. It would be backed by the full might of the state: police, civil servants, prison wardens, judges, lawyers. This time, the pillars of German society would not just stand aside. They would be active participants.

But one thing didn't change. Hitler and Goebbels encouraged the Brownshirts in extreme but vague language, which was then translated by the foot soldiers into violent action. 'The beacon in Berlin, signs of fire all over the country,' one stormtrooper recounted. 'Finally the relief of the order: "Go to it."'

In towns and cities across Germany, the Brownshirts burst forth onto the streets, on foot and in motor cars, armed to the hilt, the police beside them. Communist offices were destroyed and officials taken into custody. Some were prosecuted in formal criminal courts, others were beaten to within an inch of their lives, or thrown in to makeshift torture chambers and impromptu prisons, or simply murdered on the spot. By the end of the year, officials of the banned Communist Party estimated that 2,500 of their members had been killed and 130,000 imprisoned. Even at this stage, with their German comrades crushed, the Comintern in Moscow absurdly insisted: 'The establishment of the open fascist dictatorship . . . is accelerating the rate of Germany's advance towards the proletarian revolution.'

The first civil liberties were suspended even as the Reichstag still smouldered. On the morning after the fire, Hitler presented a decree to cabinet that removed the individual rights of the Weimar era. 'The psychologically correct moment for the confrontation has now arrived,' he said. 'There is no purpose in waiting any longer for it.' Freedom of expression, assembly and association were abolished. Police were allowed to detain people in custody indefinitely without a court order. It is extraordinary that despite all this propaganda and intimidation, the Nazis still only won 43.9 per cent of the vote in the federal elections on 5 March. It is useful to remember that an absolute majority of the German people never voted for them.

The final killing stroke against the Weimar Republic came in the form of the Enabling Act, which amended the constitution so that Hitler could bypass the Reichstag and the president entirely. It would need to be renewed every four years, but everyone understood that this would be a mere formality. On 23 March, at the Reichstag's new home in the Kroll Opera House, Hitler announced the Act to the gathered deputies underneath a huge swastika banner. The Social Democrat deputies were taunted by young men who called them, confusingly, both 'centrist pig' and 'Marxist sow'. Hitler made it clear that any resistance would be met by death: 'May you, gentlemen, now take the decision yourselves as to whether it is to be peace or war.'

If anyone emerged from this time of cruelty and cowardice with any dignity, it was the Social Democrats. 'In this historic hour, we German Social Democrats solemnly profess our allegiance to the basic principles of humanity and justice, freedom and socialism,' said party chairman Otto Wels, with a cyanide capsule in his pocket in case he was arrested. 'We greet the persecuted and the hard-pressed . . . The courage of their convictions, their unbroken confidence, vouch for a brighter future.' As this German Matteotti spoke, mocking laughter filled the chamber.

Only the Social Democrats voted against the Act. On 21 June, the party was banned and some 3,000 officials were arrested. Then the Catholic Centre Party was closed down through a concordat with Rome, agreed on 1 July. Over the next few years, Catholicism was largely driven from public life by surveillance, censorship, banning orders, arrests and imprisonment.

The other, smaller parties left over from the Weimar years were easily cleared up. Germany had become a one-party state. This was all done, in Hitler's breathless words, in the name of 'the people'. But in fact these parties represented far more voters than had ever supported the Nazis in a free election.

Hitler never ran out of enemies to persecute. Like Mussolini, he was determined to remove any potential challengers from the ranks of his fellow travellers on the right. There were two major figures of concern. Franz von Papen, the tiresome authoritarian who had never given up his dream of establishing a conservative dictatorship, was now forming connections with the army. And Ernst Röhm, the frumpy, sadistic leader of the Brownshirts, was slowly creating his own cult of personality. Like the impatient *squadristi*, he entertained the notion of a 'second revolution', with the Brownshirts in the vanguard. By this stage, the group was nearly 3 million men strong. 'Germany will become National Socialist, or it will die,' Röhm declared. 'And that is why the German Revolution continues.' But he made the fatal mistake of underestimating the man he disdained as 'the ridiculous corporal'.

Hitler decided to cut both Röhm and Papen out of the picture at the same time. The action was timed for 30 June 1934, a date that would afterwards be known as the Night of the Long Knives. In a complex, multifaceted and highly structured exercise, he murdered his way through the authoritarian social milieu.

Hitler himself took care of Röhm. Early in the morning, he arrived in a convoy of SS bodyguards and police at the Hanselbauer hotel in Bad Wiessee and marched into Röhm's room with a whip in his hand and two armed detectives at his side. 'Röhm, you are under arrest,' he shouted. Röhm looked up sleepily from his pillow and replied: 'Hail, my leader.' He was arrested along with all the other Brownshirts in the hotel.

Röhm was visited in his cell by two SS officers, who handed him a loaded Browning pistol and told him to kill himself within the next 10 minutes. When they returned, he was standing proud, his chest bared, attempting to demonstrate his sense of honour. Without a word, they shot him at point-blank range. Other Brownshirts were imprisoned, sent to concentration camps or driven to nearby forests and shot. So much for the German Revolution.

Back in Berlin, Göring was orchestrating a bloodbath. With the SS leaders Reinhard Heydrich and Heinrich Himmler, he worked his way through a kill list while striding back and forth. 'Shoot them down,' he would say into the phone. 'Shoot . . . shoot at once.' The three men would break into wild laughter every time a report of a murder came in.

Papen was not killed – he was too prominent – but he was confined to house arrest while his allies were liquidated. There was also some housekeeping to be done from Nazism's early years. Kurt von Schleicher, Hitler's predecessor as chancellor, was shot dead along with his wife at their home. Gregor Strasser, author of many of the party's institutions and former leader of the Nazi left, was shot. Gustav Ritter von Kahr, the Bavarian politician who had thwarted the Beer Hall Putsch, was taken to Dachau concentration camp and killed. Otto Ballerstedt, who had been beaten up on stage in one of Hitler's very first operations as Nazi leader back in 1921, was shot in the back of the head. Unlike Röhm, most of these men posed no danger at all. This was a bloody spasm of spite and revenge.

Altogether, at least 85 people were killed. International politicians, including Mussolini, were horrified by the massacre, but the German public largely welcomed it as a guarantee of stability.

While Hitler was eradicating any group that might stand up to the regime, he was also establishing a system of control that would stretch from the smallest apartment block to the heights of power. It would police the tiniest infraction, the smallest hint of disobedience. It aimed to obliterate the free-thinking individual.

When President Hindenburg died of lung cancer on 2 August 1934, a hastily written cabinet decree merged the offices of chancellor and president. Hitler now wielded complete power over German political life. 'The authority of the leader is total and all-embracing,' concluded the constitutional lawyer Ernst Rudolf Huber. 'Within it all resources available to the body politic merge; it covers every facet of the life of the people . . . The leader's authority is subject to no checks or controls; it is circumscribed by no private preserves of jealously guarded individual rights.' The regime usually maintained the fiction of passing legislation, but Werner Best, a Nazi jurist, believed Hitler's verbal utterances were considered legally binding by virtue of his position as embodiment of the *Volk*.

This was a level of power far in excess of anything Mussolini could achieve. In Italy, the Duce struggled to control his own party, had to manage the king, and ended up working alongside state institutions. In Germany, Hitler's mastery over the Nazi Party was total. And the state soon submitted to his will. This was totalitarianism unbound.

The anti-Nazi political scientist Ernst Fraenkel's seminal 1941 book *The Dual State* laid out a theory of how Germany operated under the Nazis. On the one hand, it featured a 'normative state' bound by rules and procedures – the courts, the Reich Chancellery, the government ministries. And on the other, it had a dark twin – the 'prerogative' system of rampant party power, operating under the Führer's personal authority. In practice, though, the prerogative state quickly subsumed the normative state. Civil servants, teachers, judges, lawyers and state employers were soon drafted into Nazi assaults on minority groups and forced to give the 'German greeting' of 'Heil Hitler' when conducting official business.

At the same time, the Nazi regime attempted to mould German society into its idealised image of the *Volk* – a unified whole defined by strength, conformity and racial purity. The Nazi term for this process of complete social and institutional control was *Gleichschaltung*, meaning coordination. 'The era of individualism finally died,' Goebbels wrote. 'The individual will be replaced by the community of the people.'

The chief transmission agent for *Gleichschaltung* was of course Hitler, who functioned as the lodestar of the nation. His message was pitched in religious language, as a kind of secular Christianity in which he played the role of the redeemer. 'I cannot divest myself of my faith in my *Volk*,' he said in a speech at the Berlin Sports Palace in February 1933. Together, he promised, they would create 'the new German kingdom of greatness and power and glory and justice. Amen.'

Hitler's new religion meant the mechanisation of humankind, with vast, elaborate expressions of obedience and sacrifice of the self. As Charlie Chaplin put it in his 1940 anti-Nazi satire *The Great Dictator*, the goal was to create 'machine men with machine minds and machine hearts'. Hannah Arendt argued that millions of Germans felt alienated and isolated by modern life and welcomed the opportunity to surrender themselves to a grand unifying project. Horrifically brainless though it looked from the outside, it felt good to belong – to break free from the responsibility of thinking for themselves.

The Nuremberg rally in 1934, involving over a quarter of a million people, was filmed by Leni Riefenstahl as *Triumph of the Will* – one of the most influential documentaries of all time. In a typical combination of fascism's melding of old and new, it deployed groundbreaking techniques like the telephoto lens and wide-angle photography to emphasise ancient iconography and promote Hitler's mystical bond with the German people. After a text proclaiming Germany's 'rebirth', the first shot shows Hitler arriving in a plane, its shadow casting a cross on the awestruck throng below. That year, the Nazi swastika became Germany's new national flag. 'The Party is Hitler and Hitler is Germany just as Germany is Hitler!' Rudolf Hess breathlessly declared.

At this stage, the two fascist dictators were simultaneously rewriting the art of tyranny in the age of mass media. Italo Calvino observed that Mussolini's 'image was more effective and tangible when seen in the cinema than it was when viewed directly by the crowd beneath that balcony'. In 1937, Mussolini opened Cinecittà Studios in Rome, the largest film studio in Europe. 'To-day the film is the strongest available weapon,' he said.

Hitler's philosophy of propaganda was founded on contempt for his audience. 'The powers of the masses are very restricted, and their understanding feeble,' he wrote in *Mein Kampf*. 'On the other hand, they quickly forget. Such being the case, all effective propaganda must be confined to a few bare essentials and those must be expressed as far as possible in stereotyped formulas.' The Nazis pushed their message right into Germans' living rooms using the radio. The entire industry, from broadcasters to engineers, was forced to belong to the Reich Radio Chamber, giving Goebbels' Propaganda Ministry total control over its output. Manufacturers were subsidised to make cheap radios known as the People's Receiver. By 1939, over 70 per cent of households had a radio – a higher percentage than any other country.

Both dictators were obsessed with architecture. Mussolini considered it the greatest of all art forms and established the fascist style as an imposing merger of Roman classicism and modernism. Fascist buildings such as the Foro Mussolini, a sports complex in Rome, were intimidatingly large, with sharp edges and minimal decoration. New roads were built in the capital, and old buildings demolished, to highlight the grandeur of Roman landmarks such as the Colosseum and the Piazza of Emperor Augustus. The city of Rome doubled in size.

Hitler's lifelong fascination with architecture gave it an even more pivotal role in Germany. Indeed, no area of German life, except perhaps war preparation, took up more of his attention. He could now take his superficial obsession with buildings, which had previously been restricted to unsold postcards, and apply it to the country's entire urban vision. He took to the project with gusto, alongside his favourite architect, Paul Troost, and then, when he died, his younger collaborator, Albert Speer. Every city, town and village in Germany had an Adolf Hitler Street.

The old party headquarters in Munich was turned into a monumental Leader Building and Administration Building, emblazoned with swastikas and eagles. One commentator described it as 'ideology become stone'. A new Reich Chancellery was commissioned in Berlin, along similar lines. Outside, the style was pseudo-classical but, inside, these buildings were fitted with modern technology, including air conditioning. Above all, they conveyed what the historian Richard J. Evans called 'maniacal gigantism': that same sense, found in Hitler's old paintings, of power and solidity in a changing world. It was an almost childlike fantasy: bigger, stronger, more.

Another new building, the Olympiastadion, was the site of Nazism's greatest public relations coup: the 1936 Berlin Summer Olympics. With violence and antisemitism strategically paused, the event successfully whitewashed both Germany and its leader. The *New York Times,* which had evidently learned nothing from its earlier misreading of Hitler's ambitions, claimed that the Olympics had 'made the

Germans more human again . . . They have seen here for themselves that all races are good.' This was arguably Hitler's peak. From then on, he believed the slogan introduced at the 1936 Nuremberg rally: 'The Führer is always right.'

In Italy, likewise, fascists proclaimed: 'Mussolini is always right.' Propaganda spun the myth of Il Duce as a wise, all-powerful father to the nation whose decisions were infallible. During the 1930s, the Fascist Party boomed under a new law that made membership compulsory for anybody employed in the public sector. The fanatical, sycophantic party secretary, Achille Starace, set about 'fascisising' the population with new language and customs, and a fetish for uniforms and salutes. The fasces were added to the state insignia, and an alternative calendar was launched, starting from the day Mussolini became prime minister. Starace even insisted that Mussolini be referred to in print in block capitals: 'DUCE'.

For all that, Mussolini and Starace never succeeded in thoroughly fascisising the Italian people. Hitler was far more effective in Germany. By 1938, virtually all opinion in society – from journalism to music, architecture to landscaping – reflected that of the regime at a granular level. Advertising and design adopted its visual tropes so that even toothpaste tubes and eggcups were emblazoned with the swastika. In gardening, foreign plants went out of fashion, to be replaced with native species. Any form of art that did not conform to fascist values – atonal music, abstract painting, 'degenerate' literature – had been purged and banned.

Control of education was fundamental to Nazism, as Hitler turned schools into laboratories for the New Man. All dictatorships seek to suppress opposition, but the Nazis wanted to eliminate the mental capacity for dissent. In almost every classroom, a portrait of the Führer glared at primary school children as they recited verses like: 'My leader! I know you well and love you like my mother and father. I will always obey you like I do my father and mother.' Educational disciplines were systematically Nazified to focus on Hitler's obsessions: German heroism in history, 'living space' in geography, 'race hygiene' in biology, and military issues like ballistics and aerodynamics in physics. Even mathematics was twisted into a kind of fascist numeracy. One test question read: 'The proportion of nordic-falian blood in the German people is estimated as $4/5$ of the population. A third of these can be regarded as blond. According to these estimates, how many blond people must there be in the German population of 66 million?'

The core of the child indoctrination programme was the Hitler Youth. Well before membership became a legal necessity in 1939, it had become all but impossible for parents to resist enrolling their children. The purpose of the organisation was, in Hitler's words, to 'burn the racial sense and racial feeling into the instinct and the intellect, the heart and brain of the youth'.

The curious thing about this obsessive restructuring of German life was that Hitler himself was a fundamentally lazy man. Whereas Mussolini was a workaholic control freak – at one point in 1929, he personally held eight cabinet posts – Hitler was happy to delegate the day-to-day business of government to his loyal lieutenants while he focused on public-facing work such as speeches at rallies. Far from the Nazi image of hyper-discipline, he lived like a student bohemian – rising late in the morning, going to sleep long past midnight, and spending much of the intervening time watching popular films. He effectively returned to his original role in the German Workers' Party as the movement's 'drummer': he set the tempo. Trusted officials were free to improvise their own initiatives as long as they kept to the Führer's rhythm.

Fascism's complicated relationship with left and right was evident in its economic policy. Mussolini spent vast amounts of money on social welfare, affordable housing and Europe's largest public works programme, including schools, hospitals, bridges and roads. In the early 1930s, the Great Depression brought about mass nationalisation of industries in Italy, second only to the USSR. The Irish socialist playwright George Bernard Shaw wrote to a friend that Mussolini's policies went 'further in the direction of Socialism than the English Labour Party could yet venture if they were in power'. Mussolini sometimes compared his strategy to the interventionist prescriptions of John Maynard Keynes and to President Roosevelt's New Deal, but he preferred more martial language: the Battle of the Grain, the Battle for Land, the Battle of the Lira. Economics to him was a form of war.

After sacking de' Stefani in 1925, Mussolini's new economic strategy was corporatism, a 'Third Way' between capitalism and socialism that aimed to submerge class tensions by bringing together businesses with fascist trade unions to set wages and prices. But really corporatism was a mirage: business interests always dominated. And the economy was nowhere near as strong as it looked.

Hitler's economic 'miracle' was also overstated. When he attained power, the global economy was already starting to recover. There was less demand for jobs due to smaller birth cohorts in the war years, and pre-existing work programmes were simply rebadged so they could be presented as the Nazis' own accomplishments. Nonetheless, new jobs programmes were introduced, most notably for motorway construction, which helped reduce unemployment. It seemed like a triumph for Nazi Keynesianism.

This was coupled with a genuinely new approach to class status. The criteria for success under Nazism were zealous ideological commitment, conformity and aggression. This meant that members of the lower classes were often elevated over those from the bourgeoisie. Professionals who had once enjoyed a high social status, like university lecturers or doctors, found themselves falling down the pecking order in a society that valued strength and discipline more than intellect and compassion. The men in charge – from Hitler and Goebbels down to the lowly block warden – were often from humbler backgrounds. 'We are the first country in Europe to overcome the class struggle,' said Robert Ley, head of the German Labour Front.

But this social overhaul did not extend to meaningful economic redistribution. Existing patterns of income and wealth were largely unaffected by Nazi rule. The tax system stayed mostly unchanged, except in the case of Jews. The rich stayed rich, the poor stayed poor and the aristocracy kept the land.

Even the work programmes were not truly Keynesian. Keynes's whole economic vision was about stimulating consumer demand in the economy with public works. But the projects the Nazis initiated involved low pay, poor working conditions, long hours and minimal food rations. There were no longer any unions to push for improvements, and those workers who did complain were sent to concentration camps. So there was no commensurate increase in the spending power of the population. The real purpose of the work programmes was not a material improvement in the life of the population. It was war.

One reason why it is so hard to define fascism is the fact that the only two fascist regimes differed in many substantial ways. Hitler looked up to Mussolini, taking from Italian fascism the Roman salute, the coloured shirts (brown rather than black) and the title of leader (Führer instead of Duce). In *Mein Kampf*, he confessed to 'a profound admiration for the great man beyond the Alps, whose ardent love for his people inspired him not to bargain with Italy's internal enemies but to use all possible ways and means in an effort to wipe them out'.

But the affection was not mutual. Mussolini avoided Hitler for as long as possible. He was instinctively anti-German, pointing out that the land had once teemed with barbarians while Rome was the centre of civilisation. He considered Nazism a 'parody of Fascism'.

When the two leaders finally met, in Venice in June 1934, Mussolini muttered: 'He's mad, he's mad.' Hitler's obsessive racism struck him as deranged. 'Instead of speaking to me about current problems,' he complained, 'he recited to me from memory his *Mein Kampf*, that enormous brick which I have never been able to read.' Mussolini was horrified by the Night of the Long Knives, sent troops into Austria to thwart a Nazi putsch, and even excluded the Nazis from a conference of international fascists in Montreux, Switzerland. He described Hitler as a 'silly little clown' and Nazism as 'barbarous and savage . . . capable only of slaughter, plunder and blackmail'. Only once Mussolini's military ambitions had shattered his relations with Britain and France would he reluctantly forge a bond with his fellow traveller.

Despite repression at home and atrocities in Libya, Italian fascism was widely associated with efficiency rather than evil. Mussolini didn't institute concentration camps, purges, book-burnings or the execution of political enemies. Astonishingly, between 1926 and 1940, only nine death sentences were passed for political offences. Each year, political prisoners numbered in the hundreds rather than the thousands. Racism and antisemitism were components of Italian fascism, but they were not foundational principles. Mussolini considered race 'a feeling, not a reality' and rejected eugenics. 'National pride has no need of the delirium of race,' he told Emil Ludwig in 1932. Not until 1938 would he make antisemitism state policy. At that point, bizarre though it seems now, one in four Italian Jewish adults belonged to the Fascist Party.

In 1941, the US journalist H. R. Knickerbocker observed: 'Mussolini's Fascist state is the least terroristic of the three totalitarian states. The terror is so mild in comparison with the Soviet or Nazi varieties, that it almost fails to qualify as terroristic at all.' The absence of mass murder on Italian soil helps to explain why Italian fascism seemed for more than a decade like a model that others could emulate. The most common argument was that even if you didn't approve of his goals or methods, you had to admit Mussolini got things done. At least, went the popular refrain, he made the trains run on time. In fact, the overhaul of the railway system had begun before he took power and local services remained unreliable. But the line accurately represents the general impression that he had turned a chaotic nation into a strong and effective modern state.

While Hitler had his own admirers abroad, Nazism was clearly something horrifyingly different.

*

At the heart of the Nazi system of control were the concentration camps. The popular notion that Hitler moved stealthily towards a terror state, hoodwinking his critics, is a fallacy. The death camps of the Holocaust came much later, but prison camps were integral to the Nazi project from the start. In August 1932, the Nazi press reported that the party would 'immediately arrest and condemn all Communist and Social Democratic functionaries . . . in concentration camps' when they came to power. They were true to their word, starting with the makeshift prisons and torture basements that emerged following the Reichstag fire.

The formalisation of this network began in March 1933 with the establishment of the Dachau camp, just outside Munich, under the instruction of SS leader Heinrich Himmler. In June 1933, Theodor Eicke – the SS colonel who had shot Ernest Röhm – was made commandant. He imposed a strict regime with set punishments for various infractions. Beatings, for example, were no longer carried out in a haphazard fashion, but according to regulations, in front of the prisoners, and then recorded in writing. Staff were issued with an insignia for their collar: the death's head. The Dachau camp became a closed system, with its own subculture of symbols, codes and structures. Eicke was soon made inspector of the other camps springing up around Germany – at least 70 within the first few months of 1933 – and systematised the model nationwide.

Over the course of that year, at least 100,000 people were arrested, with nearly 600 of them dying in custody. Most of the camps were soon shut down as the first wave of repression, aimed at political prisoners, came to an end. But in 1936, a new phase began, this time aimed at 'undesirable' elements. This came to include habitual criminals, the long-term unemployed, so-called 'deviants', 'racial degenerates' and 'asocials'

– a catch-all category that eventually incorporated prostitutes, Roma, tramps, beggars and anyone else considered pollutants of the Aryan race. The Nazis ultimately murdered up to half a million Romani people.

An inverted triangle was put on the left breast of prisoners' striped uniforms: black for asocial, red for political, violet for Jehovah's Witnesses, pink for gay men. Jews were designated as one of these categories – usually political – but with an additional yellow triangle stitched underneath, the right way up, so that it formed a perverse Star of David. Unlike other persecuted groups, the Jews were considered not just a contaminant of the master race, but an *enemy* race: the great opponents of the *Volk*, who had sought to undermine Germany at every stage.

The camps were not only a tool of control for the people inside them. They also encouraged conformity across society. Their existence was not hidden – in fact, it was widely reported in the press – but the exact nature of what went on in them was a carefully guarded secret, with guards telling released inmates that any revelation would ensure that they were brought back. This created a palpable sense of fear and compliance in the public. The ominous air of mystery around the camps and the shattered, beaten look of those who emerged from them was possibly more terrifying than any of the specific details would have been.

This fear was magnified by the secret police, or Gestapo. The organisation took on an almost mythical status, as an all-seeing eye of the state that could detect any expression of protest, no matter how minuscule: a joke against Nazis in the pub, a hint of criticism in a letter. Even a speck of discontent was treated harshly, because it was a refutation of the Nazi Party's central proposition: that race leadership had created a homogenised nation in which the individual will had been replaced by that of the Führer. To allow one mocking word to be spoken against one minor Nazi figure would challenge the philosophical basis of fascism.

'Everyone cringes with fear,' the Jewish professor Victor Klemperer wrote in his diary on 19 August 1933. 'No letter, no telephone conversation, no word on the street is safe any more. Everyone fears the next person could be an informer.' Nazism's totalising logic meant that it could not leave its citizens alone. As Robert Ley boasted: 'The only person who is still a private individual in Germany is somebody who is asleep.' Surveillance chilled the workplace, where employers, foremen, officials from the Nazi Labour Front and members of the Nazi Security Service kept watch. It even infiltrated homes, where an army of two million 'block wardens' was assigned to spy on groups of households. 'Do you know what fear is?' an elderly German asked his interviewer after the war was over. 'No. The Third Reich was fear.' But the terror would not have been sustainable without the enthusiasm of the informers, bullies, fanatics and opportunists.

Meanwhile, the regime pursued a programme of social engineering to eradicate those they deemed inferior. The 1933 Law for the Prevention of Hereditarily Diseased Offspring introduced compulsory sterilisation for those suffering from any number of issues, including schizophrenia, manic depression, epilepsy, deafness, blindness, severe physical deformity, alcoholism and so-called 'feeble-mindedness' – a dangerously broad and hazily defined concept. By the time the Third Reich ended, over 360,000 people had been sterilised. In many cases, the victims were people who had no physical or mental disability at all, but simply did not conform to the Nazi view of societal acceptability: beggars, sex workers, the

of its enemies and the radical restructuring of the state. But once that had been achieved, fascism had no excuses for not delivering on its grandiose pledges. Failure would disillusion the public and allow for rivalrous dissent within the party. Predicated on urgency, vigour and radical action, fascism could not slow down. To stop was to stagnate, probably into a typical conservative dictatorship. It was like the shark in the Woody Allen joke: it had to keep moving or it would die. And the only way for it to keep moving was to go to war.

CHAPTER FOUR
Fascism at War

Fascism was the child of war: born of it, moulded by it, obsessed with it. The First World War had given the movement motive, opportunity and a taste for blood. War was not a chance outcome of its political agenda but the inevitable consequence. Fascism *was* war.

'Three cheers for the war,' Mussolini wrote in 1921. 'Three cheers for Italy's war and three cheers for war in general. Peace is hence absurd or rather a pause in war.' During the 1930s, he came to believe that only conflict could replenish fascism's energies. He was also jealous of Hitler's place in the vanguard of fascism – the lunatic upstart who had come to define it around the world.

Mussolini became obsessed with *spazio vitale* (vital space). He believed – wrongly but not uniquely – that economic growth required territorial expansion, and claimed that Italy had every right to seize land in Africa from 'inferior' peoples. Fascist foreign policy was social Darwinist: strong nations had a right to subjugate weak ones. He wanted to aggrandise himself with the status of a military leader. 'War is to men as maternity is to women,' he declared in 1934, the year he began posing in uniform, his head encased in the Royal

Italian Army's new dome-like helmet. Revealing his strange contempt for the Italian people, he believed that only war could transform 'a gesticulating, chattering, superficial and carnivalesque country' into a great power.

Abyssinia (now Ethiopia) was the obvious prize. Bordering the colonies of Italian Eritrea and Italian Somaliland, it had been the site of a notorious military humiliation in 1896, when the Abyssinians defeated the Italian invaders at the Battle of Adua. Part of Mussolini's personal mythology was the idea that he was the man who could succeed where previous Italian leaders had failed. Racist towards Africans, he considered Abyssinia a 'barbarian country' that cried out for Italy's civilising influence, and began plotting its seizure as early as 1932.

He finally announced the invasion on 3 October 1935, mobilising half a million Italian troops. Within three days, they were in Adua, but at a severe cost to Mussolini's international reputation. The Stresa Front, Italy's anti-Hitler alliance with Britain and France, collapsed after just a few months. The League of Nations initiated economic sanctions against Italy. There would be no more glowing testimonials to his statesmanship from foreign leaders.

As they had done in Libya, Italian forces rained mustard-gas bombs on soldiers and civilians and carried out mass executions. In May 1936, they seized the Abyssinian capital, Addis Ababa. Abyssinia's *negus* (emperor), Haile Selassie, fled to England, and Mussolini became the new master of 13 million Abyssinians. But for all that effort, he had no idea what to do with his prize. He utterly failed to exploit the economic resources of his new colonies, or even to visit Abyssinia. He simply wanted to possess them.

The fascists then began a monstrous campaign of violence.

Abyssinia's sadistic new viceroy, Rodolfo Graziani, instituted a form of apartheid, executed prisoners of war en masse and brutalised the civilian population. In September 1937, after he survived an assassination attempt, his Blackshirts rampaged through Addis Ababa, burning thousands of buildings and massacring an estimated 20,000 people: one in five of the city's population. Between 1935 and 1938, Italy killed at least a quarter of a million Abyssinians. But Mussolini was unrepentant. He summed up his foreign policy philosophy: 'I want to make a cynical declaration: in international relations there is only one moral: success. We were immoral when we assailed the Negus. We won and we have become moral.'

Of course, Britain and France had committed numerous atrocities while building and sustaining their own empires. 'Your own imperial history does not entitle you to display so much concern for the independence of the Ethiopians,' Mussolini taunted a British journalist. But Italy was too late to the game. Brute-force colonialism had gone out of fashion. The new British foreign secretary, Anthony Eden, loathed Mussolini as a 'complete gangster'.

Having thrown away his two preferred allies, Mussolini was forced to strengthen ties with Hitler, a man he distrusted, derided and even despised. He signed a 1936 treaty, which he dubbed the Rome–Berlin 'axis', but not until September 1937 did he make his first visit to Berlin. Even now, with Hitler in the ascendant, the love affair was all one-way. In front of a million-strong crowd, Hitler hailed his Italian ally as 'one of those rare geniuses who make history, and are not made by it!'

In Italy, at least, the Abyssinian war had achieved its purpose. 'Finally, Italy has its empire,' Mussolini declared from a balcony in Rome, invoking the capital's glory days. His biographer Renzo De Felice called the war Mussolini's 'masterpiece'. As Il Duce had hoped, the war had rejuvenated both the fascist spirit and his own authority. Many Italian fascists, including Mussolini's sons Vittorio and Bruno, had found the experience of killing Abyssinians an invigorating adventure. At home, the war effort justified a more centralised economy and further fascisisation of Italian society. Propaganda reached a hysterical peak. Schoolteachers now wore black shirts and required their pupils to recite a 'Prayer to the Duce'. In 1939, Mussolini replaced parliament with a new Chamber of Fasces and Corporations. The Fascist Party had 2.6 million members, and half the population belonged to some kind of fascist organisation. It was the high-water mark of Italian fascism.

Mussolini had no idea that the only way was down. He had become addled by the cult of the Duce, comparing himself to Napoleon and Julius Caesar. Still a journalist at heart, he confused slogans with policy and propaganda with reality. Though increasingly inconsistent, he constructed an echo chamber of sycophantic mediocrities who would endorse whatever he said. He took personal responsibility for all three armed forces and rarely consulted his chiefs of staff. Anybody who voiced criticism was sacked. 'He thinks from now on he is God,' his former rival Italo Balbo complained. 'He has lost contact with the country and no one can make him listen to reason any more.'

Mussolini was eager for another war. 'Whoever stops is lost,' he said. On 17 July 1936, a cabal of right-wing generals mounted a coup against the left-wing Spanish Republic, commencing the Spanish Civil War. While Hitler's military contribution was modest, Mussolini supported General Francisco Franco with vast amounts of equipment and air power and 40,000 troops. Many *squadristi*, no longer required to crack heads at home, relished the opportunity to butcher leftists in Spain, while the Italian air force bombed Barcelona. Flushed with excitement, Mussolini did not care that the intervention was costly and unpopular, with unclear advantages. 'When Spain is finished I will think of something else,' he declared in 1937. 'The character of the Italian people must be moulded by fighting.'

It seems remarkable that the rest of the world was so naïve about Hitler's territorial ambitions for so long. After all, he had laid them out perfectly clearly in *Mein Kampf*. Hitler argued that Germany was overpopulated and could not feed itself from its own resources. This problem could only be solved by expansion into Central and Eastern Europe to secure new living space and access to raw materials and foodstuffs. This living space, or *Lebensraum*, was equivalent to Mussolini's *spazio vitale*, but Hitler's mission was on an altogether different scale. The first step would be to absorb Austria, and then Czechoslovakia. Then the country would engage in a war of conquest of Eastern Europe. This would suffice for 'about one to three generations', Hitler believed, before further expansion would be necessary. War provided the end goal of fascist thought and the ultimate manifestation of its worship of strength and violence. As Hitler told his generals: 'Close your hearts to pity. Act brutally. The stronger man is right.'

War radicalised both fascist regimes. It provided a space, geographically and legally, for fascism to degenerate to its logical conclusion. It allowed for the unrestrained expression of Nazism's racial hatred. 'The war . . . made possible for us the solution of a whole series of problems that could never have been solved in normal times,' Hitler admitted.

Hitler's supposedly Keynesian public works were really a way to camouflage military spending so that he could side-step the Versailles restrictions. Automobile factories could be converted to producing military vehicles, passenger planes could be turned into bombers. Rearmament costs soared from 1.5 per cent of national income in 1933 to 21 per cent in 1938.

This served to highlight the distinction between fascism and traditional conservatism. Until now, Nazism and big business seemed to have developed a mutually beneficial relationship. Hitler had destroyed the communist threat, and large companies had profited handsomely from the creation of a German war machine. The chemical and pharmaceutical conglomerate I. G. Farben, for instance, was pivotal in the government's plans due to its development of synthetic fuel and hydrogenated coal.

But big business and Nazism had very different objects of desire. The former was concerned with profits and an efficient market, the latter was obsessed with the glory of the racial soul. When the fiscally conservative president of the Reichsbank, Hjalmar Schacht, voiced concerns about military expenditure in January 1939, he was sacked. On 15 June, all limits on the printing of money were removed. A series of laws governing credit, mortgages, loans and banks curtailed the freedom to invest in anything except rearmament. By this stage, preparation for war had made war a necessity. Germany was spending so much that the only possible economic solution was the conquest of other countries and their absorption into the Reich economy.

Hitler made his first move in the Rhineland, a patch of western Germany that had been demilitarised by Versailles. On 7 March 1936, he triumphantly told the Reichstag that German troops had entered the territory that morning. 'They spring, yelling and crying, to their feet,' reported American journalist William L. Shirer, writing with the tremor of a man surrounded by maniacs. 'Their hands are raised in slavish salute, their faces now contorted with hysteria, their mouths wide open, shouting, shouting, their eyes, burning with fanaticism, glued on the new god, the Messiah.'

France could have crushed the operation, but nobody wanted to start a war over the violation of a treaty that was now widely considered unfair. Hitler got away with it. And with this victory, achieved effortlessly and without resistance, he became increasingly convinced that he was a strategist of unparalleled brilliance.

In 1938, his attention turned to Austria. Generations of pan-German nationalists had dreamed of unifying the countries into a German-speaking whole. Now Hitler would accomplish this *Anschluss* (joining) with a single order. At 5.30 a.m. on 12 March 1938, German troops crossed the border, cheered by crowds shouting 'Heil Hitler'. Flowers were thrown at their feet. Even Social Democrat agents had to confess that the admiration for Hitler in Germany was at this point bordering on the universal. 'The jubilation knew almost no bounds any more,' they reported. 'Even sections of society that had been cool towards Hitler up to this point, or rejected him, were now carried along by the event.'

Czechoslovakia was next. In May, Hitler told his generals he was 'utterly determined that Czechoslovakia should disappear from the map'. This time, there would be no flowers or beaming faces when German troops arrived. Czechoslovakia was sovereign, democratic and – outside of its three million Sudeten Germans – implacably opposed to Hitler. It had a well-trained army and an alliance with France that obliged Britain to intervene in the event of a German invasion.

But even as it hastily rearmed, Europe was still desperate to avoid conflict. In a series of high-stakes talks, British prime minister Neville Chamberlain forced Czechoslovakia to give way, handing the Sudetenland to Hitler. Nazi troops marched into the territory on 1 October 1938, with the Gestapo and SS following behind. They began throwing opponents into concentration camps and tormenting Czech Jews.

For Hitler, the Sudetenland wasn't enough. In March 1939, Emil Hácha, the elderly Czech president, went to Berlin, where Göring informed him that German bombers would be attacking Prague within a few hours. The president collapsed and had to be revived by Hitler's personal doctor. He was then told to phone the capital and order troops not to fire on the invaders. German troops moved into the country at 6 a.m. 'I shall enter history as the greatest German of them all,' Hitler said.

It says something about fascism's inherent nationalist paranoia that its two regimes were so slow and reluctant to come together. As late as early May 1939, Chamberlain and his foreign secretary, Lord Halifax, were still hoping to woo Mussolini away from Hitler. But Mussolini had decided that Britain was decadent and bourgeois ('people who carry an umbrella can never found an empire') whereas Hitler was a man of destiny. He also had more to fear from Germany. Italy's cakewalk invasion of Albania in April 1939 was partly intended as a message to Hitler: don't push me around.

'Fascism is the fightingest word in the world today,' declared *Life* magazine in 1938. 'To free peoples, it means War and Tyranny.' But Mussolini only loved wars that were easy to win. After all, they were expensive. One third of government expenditure was devoted to the armed forces, while punitive sanctions stifled foreign trade. Mussolini's various economic 'battles' had in fact been lost, producing a weak and inert economy that was not remotely prepared for a major conflict. Nor had he come close to winning the 'Battle for Births': his goal of growing the population from 40 to 60 million. His repeated claim that Italy had eight million men ready to fight was out by a factor of ten.

'There is no evidence that Italy's standard of living, which is lowest of the major powers, has been raised one jot or tittle since Il Duce came to power,' *Life* remarked. The Italian people were increasingly disillusioned with fascism, associating it with broken promises, corruption, bigotry, war and Nazism. When Mussolini's speeches were shown in cinemas, jeers and laughter could now sometimes be heard. Fascism's popularity was real while it lasted, but it had shallow roots.

Mussolini was in a tight spot – manacled to Hitler out of necessity but nervous about being dragged into a war he didn't want. On 22 May 1939, he signed a 'Pact of Steel' with Germany promising mutual military support, but he made it clear that Italy wouldn't be ready for war in Europe before late 1942 at the earliest. Neither the king nor the armed forces nor the fascists nor the people wanted one. Almost until the last minute, Mussolini was trying to dissuade Hitler from invading Poland.

He was torn over what to do if that happened: pride and history told him that breaking a pact and choosing neutrality would make him just like the weaklings he had replaced. But as his foreign minister and son-in-law Galeazzo Ciano noted, 'he sees, he knows, he feels, that the people cannot be brought to make *this* war in *these* conditions'.

*

In August 1939, Hitler and Stalin did something that had previously been unthinkable: they made a deal. The Nazi–Soviet Pact guaranteed mutual non-aggression and contained a secret clause dividing East-Central Europe between the two powers. Outsiders had underestimated totalitarianism's capacity for deadly cynicism. Fascists and communists might have been demonising each other for the last 20 years, but the two leaders weren't about to let ideology stand in the way of carving up Poland. Mussolini's early diagnosis of Stalin as a 'cryptofascist' had been confirmed. With the signing of the pact, Poland was doomed.

On 1 September, one and a half million German troops crossed the Polish border with squadrons of bombers over-head, while the Soviet Union prepared to attack Poland from the east. Chamberlain hesitated one last time, spending a couple of days praying pointlessly for a better world than the one he inhabited, before announcing that Britain was at war with Germany. The Second World War had begun.

All of this had been laid out 14 years earlier in *Mein Kampf*. 'I think it is one of the most incredible stories in history,' the journalist Dorothy Thompson said after the invasion of Poland, 'that a man could sit down and write in advance exactly what he intended to do; and then, step by step, begin to put his plan into operation. And that the statesmen of the world should continue to say to themselves: "He doesn't really mean it! It doesn't make sense!"'

For the first time, Nazi Germany was fighting for territory rather than being handed it on a plate, but the results were scarcely any slower. Poland was totally out-equipped – on 16 September alone, it was pounded by 328,000 kilos of German bombs. The last Polish units surrendered on 6 October.

This was the first example of Hitler's *Blitzkrieg*, or

'lightning war', defined by extremely rapid advance, led by tanks and motorised divisions and supported by bombers to slaughter and terrorise enemy troops. It was a shock-and-awe strategy, which engulfed the enemy with its sheer velocity and ferocity. It translated the fascist worship of power and movement into military terms. 'Our strength,' Hitler said, 'lies in our speed and our brutality.'

Countries fell to Hitler's advance one after another, with astonishing, terrifying speed. It seemed as if nothing could stop him. At 5.25 a.m. on 9 April 1940, Nazi troops entered Denmark, causing the government to surrender less than two hours later. From there, they attacked Norway, whose king went into exile with his government on 7 June, leaving behind an order for a ceasefire.

German troops invaded Holland on 10 May and the Dutch surrendered five days later. On 28 May, Belgium capitulated. The same month, Nazi armoured divisions tore through France at an impossible pace. Combat units powered forward for three days and nights without sleep, kept awake by regular doses of amphetamines. At French army headquarters, generals burst into tears when they learned of the speed of the advance. British and French troops made a desperate, haphazard escape from the beach at Dunkirk. On 17 June, the new French prime minister, 84-year-old Marshal Philippe Pétain, announced on public radio that it was time to sue for peace.

With all of Western Europe apart from the United Kingdom in his hands, Hitler performed what he believed would be his masterstroke. At 3.14 a.m. on 22 June 1941, as anyone but Stalin might have predicted, the Führer broke the Nazi–Soviet Pact and invaded the Soviet Union. More than 3.5 million Axis troops crossed a front stretching over nearly

2,000 miles – the largest invading force in history. Some 3,600 tanks were supported by 2,700 aircraft, 600,000 motor vehicles and 700,000 field guns. The German offensive shattered the Red Army defences. For a while, it seemed the Soviet regime would crumble like so many before it. In a three-pronged attack, the German forces pushed on towards Moscow, St Petersburg and the industrial region of Ukraine, covering up to 50 kilometres a day. 'Running, running until our tongues hang out,' General Gotthard Heinrici wrote. 'Always running, running, running.'

Only wartime conditions empowered Nazism to fulfil its horrific potential. The occupied territories enabled Hitler to enact his racial ideology on a colossal scale. Poland was the test bed that would establish the model Hitler would then export to the western USSR and the Baltic states.

The Poles were considered part of the Slav race: barbaric, cowardly and mentally subnormal. German officers inculcated this prejudice in their troops during the invasion. The enslavement and ultimate extermination of this race was not just an atrocity carried out in the heat of war. It was a reason for the war. As Hitler said: 'I have issued a command – and I will have everyone who utters even a single word of criticism shot – that the aim of the war lies not in reaching particular lines but in the physical annihilation of the enemy. Thus, so far only in the east, I have put my Death's Head formations at the ready with the command to send man, woman and child of Polish descent and language to their deaths, pitilessly and remorselessly . . . Poland will be depopulated and settled with Germans.' He proudly compared himself to Genghis Khan.

Savagery was commonplace. When 50 Polish schoolboys were arrested for smashing the window of a police station, for instance, SS officers beat them with rifle butts in front of their parents and then shot 10 of them. SS task forces, police units and *Wehrmacht* soldiers killed civilians indiscriminately as they drove across Poland, often setting fire to people's homes with the inhabitants still inside. Young Poles were rounded up and shipped off to work in Germany as a slave labour force.

In the Soviet Union, such barbarism took place on a monumental scale. More than three million captured Soviet soldiers were worked, shot, frozen or starved to death. Again, this was not merely a result of the brutality of battle. It was evidence of race war. The Germans regarded Soviet prisoners not as fellow soldiers, nor even fellow human beings, but as sub-human. Of the Soviet prisoners captured by the Nazis during the war, at least 58 per cent had died by the time it was over. The mortality rates for British, French and other servicemen in German captivity, by contrast, were below 2 per cent until the final months. As the historian Timothy Snyder wrote: 'As many Soviet prisoners of war died *on a single given day* in autumn 1941 as did British and American prisoners of war over the course of the entire Second World War.'

But the worst treatment was of course reserved for the Jews. Hitler's ultimate aim, as he had made clear since 1921, was the elimination of the Jewish race. That was the project he pursued most zealously in the legal no-man's-land of occupied Eastern Europe.

Hatred of the Jews highlights one of the chief distinctions between Mussolini and Hitler. The Italian leader did not embrace antisemitism until 1938, very late in the day, through the medium of class prejudice rather than racism. Although the middle classes had enabled fascism, Mussolini retained his working-class socialist contempt for the bourgeoisie. Hard-working and frugal, he despised the pampered, feckless quest for an easy life. Among his pet hates were golf, top hats and Christmas. He came to see Jews as the embodiment of bourgeois self-interest: un-fascist and un-Italian. Though he still believed that biological racism was nonsense, he publicly dressed up his pivot to antisemitism in terms that Hitler would appreciate.

The pseudoscientific 'Manifesto of Race', produced by the Council of Ministers in July 1938, claimed that Italians were in fact Aryans and Jews were therefore excluded from the nation's identity. Subsequent antisemitic laws deprived Jews of their jobs, assets and rights and created detailed registers that would later be exploited by the Nazis. Among those who left Italy as a result were Margherita Sarfatti, Mussolini's former mistress, and Enrico Fermi, the Nobel Prize-winning physicist who went on to develop America's atomic bomb. Antisemitism thus deprived the country of some of its finest minds. The racial laws shocked most Italians, as well as the Pope and several leading fascists. When one of them complained to Mussolini, he replied: 'I agree with you entirely. I don't believe a bit in the stupid antisemitic theory. I am carrying out my policy entirely for political reasons.' But it made no difference to the Jews whether he was sincere or not.

In Germany, Jews had effectively been extracted from economic, civil and social life by 1938. They had been driven out of schools and universities, denied access to the professions, and banned from any kind of relationship with non-Jews under laws prohibiting 'racial defilement'. Boycotts and violent attacks meant that by July 1938, only 9,000 Jewish shops were left in Germany out of the estimated 50,000 that had existed in 1933.

On 7 November 1938, Hitler and Goebbels found the excuse they needed for a full-blown pogrom. Herschel Grynszpan, a unemployed. It was a biological form of social control.

Hitler escalated the eugenics programme to enforced euthanasia in 1939, starting with children. 'Malformed' newborns selected for killing were sent to special wards, where they were starved to death or murdered using a sedative or an injection of morphine. One teacher visiting a killing ward at the Eglfing-Haar clinic reported that the director picked up a child and showed it to him. 'Displaying the child like a dead rabbit, he pontificated with the air of a connoisseur and a cynical smirk something like this: "With this one, for example, it will still take two to three days."' In this way, 5,000 children were murdered.

The regime then began to murder adult patients, using a new technique: the gas chamber. A project code-named Aktion T4 was developed for the killing of the mentally unwell and the disabled. The SS officer Albert Widmann built an experimental gas chamber in the old city prison at Brandenburg. It was an airtight chamber, three metres by five, lined with tiles to make it look like a shower room, so that those entering it would not panic. A gas pipe was fitted to the wall to pump in the fumes and a viewing window was installed in the door.

During the first experiment, senior officials took turns to watch through the window as eight patients were murdered. Asylums and hospitals were repurposed as killing stations, claiming tens of thousands of lives. The machinery of the Holocaust was now in place.

Fascism's relentless acceleration was compelled by the myth it had created. 'Inactivity is death,' 'The Doctrine of Fascism' declared. Its core promise to its followers was that it would violently purify a decadent nation so that it could attain its glorious destiny. Initially, that justified the brutal repression

17-year-old Polish-Jewish expatriate living in Paris, discovered that his parents had been deported from Germany to Poland. He marched into the German embassy and shot the first official he saw, a junior diplomat named Ernst vom Rath. The Nazi press immediately branded it an attack on Germany by 'world Jewry'.

When Rath died of his injuries two days later, Hitler told Goebbels to prepare a vast coordinated assault on Germany's Jews along with mass arrests. As ever, this was enacted through deniable language. 'The Reich Propaganda Leader's verbal instructions were understood by the Party leaders who were present to mean that the Party should not appear publicly as the organiser of the demonstrations, but that it should in reality organise them and carry them out,' the Party Supreme Court observed.

Soon virtually every synagogue in Germany was on fire. Jewish homes and businesses were vandalised and set alight. Jewish cemeteries were dug up and smashed. Jewish orphanages were burned, with the children forced out into the night. Jewish men were publicly humiliated in the street. The next day, school classes were brought out to spit on them. Around 30,000 Jewish men were transported to the concentration camps of Dachau, Buchenwald and Sachsenhausen, with many of them killed in random acts of sadism. This was Kristallnacht: the Night of Broken Glass.

The war vastly expanded the scope of Nazi antisemitism. Poland contained more Jews than anywhere else in Europe: 3.5 million, 2 million of whom lived in the territories Germany had conquered. They were left to face the full impact of Nazi racial extremism, in a space where no law applied, no reputational risks were heeded and no moral restraint existed.

Himmler's protégé, Reinhard Heydrich, organised seven

special SS task forces, or *Einsatzgruppen*, to operate in Poland. Hitler called Heydrich 'the Man with the Iron Heart'. His death squads began to shoot Jews indiscriminately, including children. Regular German army troops, too, unleashed years of racial indoctrination and hatred. Some Jews were put in work details so brutal that half of them died.

Eventually the Nazis settled on a process of ghettoisation, forcing Jews into concentrated areas of Polish cities. In Lodz, for instance, the ghetto was sealed on 1 May 1940, confining Jews to an area lacking in basic amenities like running water or a sewage system. In Warsaw, the ghetto was sealed off with three-metre walls and barbed wire on 16 November. 'One walks past corpses with indifference,' the Jewish historian Emanuel Ringelblum wrote. 'The corpses are mere skeletons, with a thin covering of skin over their bones.'

The initial stages of the Holocaust took place in a chaotic manner, with local initiatives spurred on by demands from Berlin. In June 1941, four *Einsatzgruppen* – designated A, B, C and D – followed the *Wehrmacht* into the Soviet Union. They were tasked with killing the 'Jewish-Bolshevist leadership cadre'. In reality, they murdered male Jews wherever they found them.

They then escalated to systematically shooting entire Jewish populations, including women and children. In Kiev in September, Task Force C massacred 33,771 Jews in the Babi Yar ravine over the course of two days. By the end of 1941, the *Einsatzgruppen* and their associated military and paramilitary groups had shot around half a million Jews.

The process reflected the core organising principles of Nazism. Hitler gave no single specific order, but he established the parameters and encouraged action through the use of annihilating rhetoric. In January 1942, for example, he said that 'the war can only end either by the Aryan peoples being exterminated or by Jewry disappearing from Europe'. Himmler and Heydrich then manifested that rhetoric in a whirlwind of repeat visits, inspections and instructions. Since the Weimar days, senior figures had been competing for Hitler's approval by showing how thoroughly they could put his demands into practice. Individual actions were carried out on the initiative of local SS commanders on the ground, as they had been by the Brownshirts a decade earlier.

Before late 1941, the Nazis had considered various options for removing Europe's Jewish population. There had been proposals to turn the island of Madagascar or a chunk of the conquered Soviet Union into a giant slave colony. Once military setbacks made mass deportations impossible, a new plan, the Final Solution, emerged: the extermination of the Jewish race. Mass shootings were not sufficient, partly because they were having a debilitating effect on the men ordered to carry them out. Many members of the *Einsatzgruppen* had proved 'unable to endure wading through blood any longer', reported SS officer Rudolf Höss, and had committed suicide. The other reason was that shooting could not kill enough people.

An alternative was provided by the Aktion T4 euthanasia programme, whose gassing technicians were now available for redeployment. Chełmno in Poland was the first camp the Nazis built for the sole purpose of mass murder. Jews were transported there from the Nazi-controlled ghetto and taken to the gassing vans, which drove 50 people at a time to woods 16 kilometres away, gassing them as they went. Some 360,000 Jews were killed in this manner.

Larger gassing operations were established, under the name Operation Reinhard, at three new camps: Bełżec,

Sobibor and Treblinka. Following the model developed during the euthanasia programme, the chamber was fitted to look like showers, with an airtight seal and pipes that supplied the engine exhaust fumes. These three camps murdered 1.7 million Jews.

A further killing station was established at a pre-existing concentration camp called Auschwitz, under Höss's command. Instead of exhaust fumes, a chemical pesticide called Zyklon B was used. Auschwitz-Birkenau became synonymous with the Holocaust because it was a labour camp (Auschwitz I) as well as a killing machine (Auschwitz II, aka Birkenau). Around 100,000 people survived the former, which is why we have so many stories about it. The institutions of Operation Reinhard, however, were exclusively 'death factories', in Timothy Snyder's words. When the camps ran out of people to kill, they were dismantled, destroying evidence of genocide. Only a few dozen Jews entered their gates and lived to talk about what happened there. One of them, Adam Krzepicki, described Treblinka as 'just earth, sky and corpses'. The death factories were black holes.

In total, around six million Jews were killed by the Nazi regime and its allies: around three million in the extermination camps, 700,000 in the mobile gas vans, 1.3 million by shooting, and up to a million from hunger, disease or conventional murder.

No other genocide in history has been carried out by mechanical means in specially constructed facilities. According to some estimates, it would have taken 200 years for pogroms to achieve what the Holocaust did in just three. It was also modern in an ideological sense. The idea of racial cleansing reflected certain ideas in eugenics, with its emphasis on science, public health and race hygiene. It represented a typically fascist combination of age-old prejudices and cutting-edge technology.

The Holocaust was not a clinical process overseen by cold, disinterested administrators. It was the product of the New Man that fascism had created. The men who operated the gas chambers had been moulded over many years to obey orders without question as a condition of race leadership and to put aside their capacity for independent thought or conscience. They had been taught that their position in the racial hierarchy entitled them to do as they pleased with inferior peoples, without scruple or hesitation, and that the more savagely and heartlessly they behaved, the better they reflected the values of their group. They had been indoctrinated in an extremist ideology that said Jews were dangerous subhumans, responsible for every misfortune that might befall them.

The Holocaust was the purest demonstration of what German fascism was. And what it was meant to be.

When the Second World War began, Mussolini stayed neutral but conflicted. 'It is humiliating to remain with our hands folded while others write history,' he grumbled to Ciano. One British diplomat compared him to a man on a diving board, reluctant to jump but too proud to climb down. Mussolini would sometimes wake up with one intention and go to sleep with another. The man of instinct and will could not make up his mind. Some leading fascists speculated that he was losing it.

Germany's unexpectedly devastating *Blitzkrieg* on France in May 1940 was the push he needed. Mussolini expected that the war would be won as early as September, and fantasised about a post-war settlement in which Italy could add the African colonies of Britain and France to its empire. He told Marshal

Pietro Badoglio, the army's chief of staff: 'I only need a few thousand dead so that I can sit at the peace conference as a man who has fought.' Such was the love he had for his people. Italy declared war on 10 June.

After coat-tailing the invasion of France at the last minute, Il Duce felt compelled to take the initiative and conduct his own parallel war, mounting invasions of Greece and Egypt. But he proved to be an incompetent and deluded war leader. Italy was beaten back in both countries and had to be bailed out by Germany, reinforcing the dangerous impression that Mussolini had turned himself into Hitler's inept sidekick.

Italy suffered a series of symbolic reversals. Italo Balbo, the former Blackshirt and governor-general of Libya, was shot down by friendly fire; Mussolini's son, Bruno, died in a training accident. In April 1941, Addis Ababa was liberated by British forces, heralding the end of Italian East Africa. Worst of all, Mussolini committed 230,000 men to Hitler's invasion of the Soviet Union, more than half of whom ended up dead or captured.

The mood on the home front was also grim. Italy's cities were pummelled by Allied bombing raids and immiserated by shortages of food and basic goods even as leading fascists secretly hoarded luxuries. Staged demonstrations in support of the war effort could not paper over massive public unrest. In the spring of 1943, strikes by more than 100,000 workers represented the first mass protest against fascism in two decades.

What was fascism without the paralysing spell of fear? Mussolini railed against the Italian people, who despite his best efforts remained shallow, treacherous cowards. 'His failure to galvanise more than a minority of Italians for a fascist war was a sign that the "new fascist man" had perhaps been an illusion, all along,' wrote the historian John Foot. 'Had the regime really been no more than speeches and parades?'

In the end, Italian fascism fell quickly. Visibly ailing, Mussolini made his final balcony speech on 5 May, two days before the surrender of Tunisia marked the end of the war in Africa. In July, General Dwight D. Eisenhower's Allied forces invaded Sicily. The days of 'The Leader is always right' were long gone. No fascist dictator can survive a military humiliation.

In the end, it was Mussolini's fellow fascists who wielded the knife. At an exhausting meeting of the Grand Council, which began on the suffocatingly hot afternoon of 24 July and ran through the night, his authority collapsed. Veteran Blackshirt and president of the chamber Dino Grandi accused him of embroiling Italy in a disastrous war and proposed a motion demanding that he surrender power to the king. Mussolini was too sick and weary to fight back. The motion passed by a margin of two to one. 'My star has grown dim,' he told his mistress, Clara Petacci.

Nobody had done more to empower Mussolini than the king; now only Victor Emmanuel had the legal authority to remove him. Later that day, he replaced Mussolini with 71-year-old Marshal Badoglio and ordered his *carabinieri* to arrest the man whose power had once seemed unquestionable. The Fascist Party was dissolved and banned.

Fascism's thesis of strength through war had been trashed. Instead, war had destroyed both fascism's credibility and its founder. In its political obituary for Mussolini, *Time* quoted famous bombastic slogans such as 'If I advance, follow me; if I retreat, kill me; if I die, avenge me.' But now, 'Benito Mussolini's people had had enough of such phrases. Of late the trains had not even run on time.'

When the news of Mussolini's removal broke on the radio,

there were celebrations in the streets. Fascist headquarters across the country were ransacked. In Bologna, 70 kilometres from Mussolini's birthplace, anti-fascists tore down and decapitated a statue of the fallen leader on horseback and paraded its head through the city before dumping it in the street.

Italy's surrender to the Allies on 3 September 1943 did not remove it from the war. Within a week, the *Wehrmacht* was in Rome and the king and prime minister had fled. Torn limb from limb, Italy became a battleground for the Germans, the Allies and bands of anti-fascist partisans. 'I spent two of my earliest years surrounded by SS, Fascists, and Resistance fighters all busily shooting at one another,' recalled the novelist and scholar Umberto Eco, who was 11 when Mussolini fell.

Mussolini, meanwhile, was rescued by the Germans from his cosy incarceration in a ski resort and installed as the head of a puppet government: officially the Italian Social Republic but popularly known as the Republic of Salò, after its headquarters on the shores of Lake Garda. Ailing and broken, he only accepted the role under duress. Yet Hitler still delusionally considered him 'my best and perhaps the only friend I have in the world'.

Italian fascism survived, then, in severely reduced circumstances. On paper Mussolini still ruled half of Italy; in practice he was just the frontman for the Nazi occupation. Far too late, he tried to return fascism to its radical roots. Ousted by the king, he revived his youthful anti-monarchism: 'It is not the regime that has betrayed the monarchy, it is the monarchy that has betrayed the regime . . . The state we want to establish will be national and social in the highest sense of the word; that is, it will be Fascist, thus returning to our origins.'

He also claimed to regret allying with big business instead

of the working classes, and introduced a new economic policy of 'socialisation', including mass nationalisations of private companies and improved workers' rights. He even said that he would have preferred to call his new regime the Italian Socialist Republic, and chose as his right-hand man Nicola Bombacci, who had been the Socialist Party leader and co-founder of the Communist Party before turning fascist.

Filippo Marinetti, the Futurist poet and first-generation fascist, recommended that Mussolini drop the word fascist altogether because it had become associated with corruption and defeat. But the movement's credibility was beyond rebranding and the new policies amounted to nothing. Salò had no power to do anything but kill.

Italy became a chaotic scramble of violence, panic and deadly recrimination. German fascists terrorised their former ally, massacring Italian soldiers who refused to fight on their side. The lists of Jewish citizens drawn up under the 1938 racial laws made it easy for the Nazis to round them up and send them to the camps. Among them was Primo Levi, a chemist from Turin who became perhaps the greatest first-person chronicler of the Holocaust.

While Italian partisans took bloody revenge on leading fascists such as Giovanni Gentile, Mussolini himself took care of five of those who had voted to depose him, including Emilio De Bono, one of the Quadrumvirs who had led the March on Rome, and Galeazzo Ciano, his own son-in-law. They were executed by firing squad in a fort in Verona in January 1944.

As the Axis forces retreated to the far north of Italy in the final months of the war, Mussolini boasted that fascism would fight to the last man and turn Milan into the 'Stalingrad of Italy', but that was merely the bombast of a doomed man. Few Italians were willing to lay down their lives for this impotent failure. On 27 April 1945, he was fleeing north towards Switzerland, disguised as a German soldier, when his convoy was stopped by partisans and he was recognised. His cult of personality had made his face far too famous for camouflage.

He was executed the following afternoon. His body was taken to Milan's Piazzale Loreto and laid out in the mud, where it was kicked, shot and spat on by angry citizens. 'Make a speech now,' taunted one man as he stuffed a dead mouse into the corpse's mouth, 'make a speech.' It was then hung upside down, alongside the body of Clara Petacci, from the bomb-damaged skeleton of an Esso service station – a final humiliation that was saturated with symbolism and memory. The piazza was less than an hour's walk from the hall where in March 1919 Mussolini had introduced fascism to the world. The ritual display of Il Duce's body was designed to signify the death of fascism and the birth of a new Italy that would never allow it to rise again.

Until the autumn of 1941, Hitler had expected the defeat of the Soviet Union to be easy. If the superior Western European races had collapsed so quickly, he thought, then the inferior Slav race would fall even faster. The USSR's cities would be demolished, its food confiscated by the Reich (an estimated 30 million people would starve to death in the first winter alone) and a swathe of its land turned into a slave colony for Europe's Jews. Such would be the nature of Hitler's empire.

But it never came to pass. Hitler and his generals disagreed about whether to press on to Moscow or strengthen the attack in the south. Once the impasse was resolved with a reinforced march on the capital, the autumn rains turned the unmade roads to muck. Without them, there were no deliveries of food, munitions or fuel. Winter then hardened the roads but delivered a pulverising Russian chill, which froze German equipment and left German troops hungry, exhausted and frostbitten. Then General Georgei Zhukov, who had been appointed to defend Moscow, turned back the *Wehrmacht*'s remorseless advance and forced it into retreat.

Between July 1942 and February 1943, the Battle of Stalingrad saw the German war machine stutter to a complete stop. Fascism's constant surging movement forward finally ended. And from the moment it did so, its internal conviction began to falter. Germany entered a period of permanent retreat, driven back through Russia, into Poland, and eventually inside its own borders.

Back home, the SS reported 'deep shock' among members of the public: 'There is a general conviction that Stalingrad signifies a turning-point in the war.' The *Gleichschaltung* system of total societal control began to break down. For the first time in many years, Hitler became a target of ridicule. 'Even national comrades who hardly know one another are exchanging political jokes,' the SS reported. 'Clearly they are assuming that anyone can tell any joke today without having to reckon with being rebuffed, let alone being denounced to the police.' One party member reported that he greeted 51 people with the words 'Heil Hitler' one morning and only two used it back.

The end of the advance on Russia was a death blow to one of Nazism's central propositions. Hitler had persistently maintained that might was right. But now, as the Nazis were beaten back by a supposedly inferior racial group, that argument collapsed in on itself. Its military failure was tantamount to ideological failure. The intellectual edifice could not stand.

This was accompanied by America's entry into the war in

Europe and a morale-destroying Allied bombing campaign against German cities. 'We find ourselves in a situation of helpless inferiority,' Goebbels wrote. Hitler himself started to retreat into his shell. 'In my earlier years, Hitler had made a habit of showing himself at the window of his special train whenever it stopped,' said Albert Speer, who had pored over architectural plans with the Führer in peacetime and then been elevated to Minister of Armaments and War Production during the war. 'Now these encounters with the outside world seemed undesirable to him; instead, the blinds on the station side of the train would be lowered.'

Even Hitler's body was rebelling against his commands. Since 1941, he had shown signs of progressive heart disease. Symptoms of a mild but worsening case of Parkinson's had started to emerge: a tremor in his left hand that grew more severe over the course of 1942, along with a growing hunch. He developed periodic stomach cramps. When he did speak publicly, which was increasingly rare, the electric quality of his oratory had faded. Like Mussolini, he could no longer play the strongman and chose to hide from his people rather than advertise his decline. Even the loyalists were shunned. His dog, Speer said, was 'the only living creature at headquarters who aroused any flicker of human feeling in Hitler'.

Towards the end, the Führer was a shadow of his former self. Whereas people had once stood immediately when he entered a room, they now remained seated and continued their conversations. 'His limbs trembled,' Speer wrote. 'His uniform . . . was often neglected in this last period of life and stained by the food he had eaten with a shaking hand.' He was reduced to playing a child's fantasy of war, trapped in his bunker conference room, moving divisions of armies that did not exist and railing against the betrayal of his generals.

After the war, the Allies would find startlingly few Germans who admitted to having been committed Nazis, even though party membership had peaked at 8.5 million. This revealed the essential emptiness of fascism – as soon as it stopped delivering success and Hitler's dark magic faded, there was no reason to believe in it. It was as if a fever had broken and millions of Germans could no longer comprehend why they had been willing to kill and die for this lunatic. Outside of the SS, fascism's New Man never really existed.

In early June 1944, Allied troops landed in Normandy and began to push their way upwards through Europe. On 20 April 1945, the Red Army opened the final assault on Berlin.

In its final days, the Nazi regime turned on its own people. The public appetite for fighting had collapsed. In fact, many Germans had grown sentimental about the First World War Armistice, whose terms had so insulted nationalists in 1918. 'What decent people Hindenburg and Ludendorff were by comparison,' one member of the public said. 'When they saw that the game was up, they brought it to an end and didn't let us go on being murdered.' That is to ignore the two men's authorship of the stab-in-the-back myth that fed the Nazi Party in the first place, but it is true that they lacked Hitler's willingness to turn Berlin into a funeral pyre. Surrender was unacceptable to the Führer, who demanded that each German fight to the last breath. In this last paroxysm of Nazi terror, up to 10,000 people were summarily executed for refusing to join his last stand. 'If the German people are not prepared to stand up for their own preservation, fine,' he said. 'Let them perish.'

On 30 April, as Soviet troops closed in on his Berlin bunker, Hitler finished lunch and went to his study with Eva Braun, his long-time mistress and wife of one day. Braun swallowed cyanide; Hitler shot himself in the head. Having just heard of

Mussolini's fate, he had left instructions that his own body be incinerated to avert a similar indignity. The two corpses were wrapped in blankets, taken upstairs and set alight. The funeral party gave one final 'Heil Hitler' and returned underground. But Hitler could not force his people to mourn him. As one woman in Hamburg reported when the news came over the radio: 'Nobody wept or even looked sad.' For Germany, the war was over. And so, it seemed, was fascism.

But President Harry Truman had a warning for the new United Nations a few weeks later. He insisted that 'fascism did not die' with Mussolini and Hitler after all: 'It is easier to remove tyrants and destroy concentration camps than it is to kill the ideas that gave them birth.'

CHAPTER FIVE
Failed Fascists

'The twentieth century will be the century of Fascism,' Mussolini announced in 1932. Mercifully, this did not prove to be the case, but during his first decade in power, Mussolini had good reason to think that he had created an irresistible template for the future. In 1925, the Italian magazine *Gerarchia* claimed there were at least 40 movements around the world 'that call themselves Fascist or are declared to be such', and that 'possibly before long a large part of Europe will become more or less fascist'.

The essayist Paul Berman observed that every fascist movement attempted to appear 'autochthonous, provincial, inimitable and ancient, stewing in its own pot and emitting its own idiosyncratic vapours from the distant past', rather than resemble a foreign import. Mussolini himself was torn over whether his invention should become a global movement. In 1928, he declared that 'fascism is not for export', even as he funnelled subsidies to fascist groups across Europe. After 1933, he competed with Hitler for influence over foreign movements. The Italians' short-lived Fascist International held conferences in Montreux in 1934 and Amsterdam in 1935. But the money was wasted. In most of Europe, fascist parties never won more than 2 per cent of the vote in national elections.

Fascism's general failure illustrates just how profoundly evitable it was. For fascism to prevail, four conditions had to be met: the apparent failure of the democratic status quo, the perceived threat of leftist revolution, a divided opposition, and the anxious complicity of conservatives, establishment figures and the middle classes. Fascism needed to be seen as the only solution to otherwise insurmountable problems.

The history of fascism outside of Italy and Germany raises a series of devilish questions. First, why did explicitly fascist movements fail in the US, UK, Europe and throughout the world? Second, were dictatorships like General Franco's in Spain or António Salazar's in Portugal effectively fascist, or did they just steal some of the trappings? This can help us establish the difference between authoritarian dictatorships and fascism and get us closer to understanding what fascism actually is.

If in 1900 you had asked a European intellectual to predict which country was most likely to produce a militaristic, antisemitic, ultranationalist regime, they would almost certainly have told you it was France. It had all the ingredients. The humiliation of the Franco-Prussian War in 1870–1 had wounded the Third Republic and inspired growing discontent. An angry convergence of royalists, Catholics, nationalists and antisemites had created an active radical right that produced the greatest volume of proto-fascist thought in Europe. And it was all supercharged by the Dreyfus Affair.

In 1894, a Jewish French army captain called Alfred Dreyfus was falsely accused of passing military documents to Germany. Over the next 12 years, his trial, imprisonment and overdue vindication divided France on a scale out of all proportion to the facts of the case: a kind of national nervous breakdown, playing out against a backdrop of violent and widespread antisemitism. Maurice Barrès, a far-right novelist and parliamentary deputy, seems to have invented the term 'national socialism' during the Dreyfus years.

The French experience epitomises the difficulty of cleanly identifying proto-fascist movements. To the right of mainstream conservatism were a variety of groups with different priorities but a shared obsession with nationalism and antisemitism. The slickest and most influential was Action Française, which inspired imitators in Spain, Portugal and Greece. Launched in 1899 by the ferocious Dreyfus-baiter Charles Maurras, it called for the downfall of the Third Republic and the restoration of both the monarchy and Roman Catholicism as the state religion. Its perceived enemies included socialists, Protestants, Freemasons and immigrants as well as Jews. Members of its youth wing engaged in street violence. The Mussolini-inspiring Georges Sorel wrote for its newspaper. The German historian Ernst Nolte described it as 'the beginning of fascism', but most scholars think it was insufficiently radical and modern. It was a phenomenon of the pre-war order.

In the aftermath of the First World War, France saw the birth of multiple groups with more pronounced fascist characteristics. The paramilitary squads of the Jeunesses Patriotes wore flashy blue raincoats and berets. War veterans founded the Croix-de-Feu, a paramilitary far-right league with serious political ambitions. Marcel Bucard's blue-shirted Mouvement Franciste was directly inspired and financed by Italian fascism. Georges Valois, founder of Le Faisceau, was even more overt, coming up with the ideological mathematics of 'nationalism plus socialism equals fascism'.

France, however, was not Italy. It was a prosperous,

victorious imperial power with a long democratic history – not ideal conditions for a fascist takeover. During the 1920s, conservatives were too strong to require fascist support. Not until the Great Depression did the French far right see an opportunity to break through. On 6 February 1934, far-right groups rioted on Paris's Place de la Concorde, bringing down prime minister Édouard Daladier. Economically battered, France had experienced twelve prime ministers in a little over four years, including four in the past five months. The fascists had taken cues from Hitler and Mussolini's paths to power. But so had the anti-fascists. Though the German left had failed to learn from Italy's mistakes, the French left had learned from Germany's. The crucial lesson was that only an alliance of communists and social democrats could defeat fascism. They bonded together as the Popular Front, swept the 1936 election under the Jewish socialist Léon Blum and promptly banned all far-right leagues.

In response, the far right polarised. Extremists calling themselves La Cagoule (the Cowl) plotted bombings and assassinations, bankrolled by businessmen including the founder of L'Oréal cosmetics. But this was a terrorist group, not a mass movement. *Time* called them the 'French Ku Klux Klan'. Former Croix-de-Feu leader Colonel François de la Rocque formed the Party Social Français (PSF), but that was reactionary, not revolutionary. There was no fascist movement to speak of.

The key moment for French fascism came in July 1940, when France's Nazi occupiers established the puppet Vichy government in the south, led by the collaborator Marshal Pétain, with the PSF slogan of 'work, family, fatherland'. The regime deported tens of thousands of Jews to concentration camps, while its brutal paramilitary force, *la Milice*, drew volunteers from pre-war far-right groups. But moral atrocity though he was, Pétain was ultimately more of an ultra-conservative in the mould of Franco and Salazar than an outright fascist. It is telling that many ardent fascists shunned Vichy and chose to live in Nazi-occupied cities such as Paris. These French nationalists could only find the purity they craved under German rule.

If one essential condition of fascism is a charismatic leader, then British fascism had one in the form of Oswald Mosley. A powerful orator with the sinister, athletic good looks of a villain in a melodrama, Mosley saw himself as the dashing hero of a great adventure. With this came the vanity and reckless arrogance that would doom him.

Like many fascists, Mosley took the long way round. An aristocrat and war veteran, he became a Conservative MP in 1918 – at 22, the youngest MP in the House – and soon built a reputation as a compelling public speaker. Firmly on the left wing of the Tories, he left the party altogether over its Irish policy in 1920 and became an independent. In 1924, he switched to the Labour Party and joined the socialist Fabian Society.

At this point, UK fascism was in its infancy. Originally called the British Fascisti, the British Fascists had been founded in 1923 in direct homage to Mussolini by Rotha Lintorn-Orman, an anti-communist war veteran and former Girl Scout from a military family. It acquired a few thousand members, including powerful figures from the armed forces and the aristocracy, a handful of Conservative MPs and, incredibly, the manager and captain of the England cricket team, but soon fractured. The fanatical antisemite Arnold Leese, who formed the Nazi-funded Imperial Fascist League in 1929, derided the British Fascists as 'conservatism with knobs on'.

Mosley dismissed them as 'black-shirted buffoons, making a cheap imitation of ice-cream sellers' – an anti-Italian slur.

Mosley was a rising star in the Labour Party and was talked about as a future prime minister. In 1929, he was appointed to Ramsay MacDonald's cabinet but became frustrated with the establishment's *laissez-faire* response to the Great Depression. He drew up a plan known as the Mosley Memorandum, with an interventionist recipe similar to that of John Maynard Keynes: nationalisation of industries, public works programmes and corporatism. This proved far too radical for the Labour leadership, and he resigned his post. After the Labour conference narrowly voted down his plan, he stormed out of the party altogether in a fit of pique and established his own New Party.

After a catastrophic wipeout in the 1931 election, Mosley responded like a typical demagogue and decided he was against parliamentary democracy in general. Forsaking his anti-Italian slurs, he journeyed to Rome, where he was captivated by Mussolini and adopted the black shirts and fasces emblem for his own British Union of Fascists (BUF). Secretly subsidised by Italy, the BUF claimed to promote 'national socialism', while its paramilitary Fascist Defence Force kept order at rallies and harassed communists in the streets. Almost all the British Fascists defected to the BUF, including William Joyce, who later became the notorious Nazi propagandist known as Lord Haw-Haw.

At first, Mosley's forceful anti-communism attracted some powerful supporters. In January 1934, Lord Rothermere, proprietor of the *Daily Mail*, wrote an article with the infamous headline: 'Hurrah for the Blackshirts!' The BUF also drew in people who should have known better, such as former suffragettes Mary Richardson and Mary Allen, who saw in the party 'the courage, the action, the loyalty, the gift of service, the ability to serve which I had known in the suffragette movement'. The vital, deadly alliance of street violence and elite endorsement was forming and the British intelligence services began monitoring Mosley as a potential threat.

Mosley's bubble burst on 7 June 1934. His rally at London's Olympia was a grand spectacle in the Nazi style, which attracted 10,000 spectators, including scores of MPs and aristocrats. But he made a serious mistake. He kept pausing his speech so that Blackshirts could set upon anti-fascist hecklers with knuckledusters and clubs. While brawls at British political meetings were nothing new, orchestrated violence was. Mosley had revealed himself as a bully.

'The Olympia meeting has at least done this service – it has demonstrated the nature of the Fascist movement to thousands of people who had hitherto been ignorant of its intentions and methods,' remarked the *New Statesman*. Three weeks later, Hitler's Night of the Long Knives offered conservatives a preview of where Mosleyism could lead – it might start with Marxists, but it could end with their heads on the block too. The likes of Rothermere quickly backed away from the BUF as party membership and rally attendance collapsed.

In a cynical attempt to revive the BUF, Mosley made aggressive antisemitism one of its core values. But in October 1936, hundreds of thousands of anti-fascists blocked a BUF march through London's East End in the so-called Battle of Cable Street. In response to the violence, the Public Order Act outlawed political uniforms in public places.

Mosley rebounded one last time in the era of appeasement under the slogan 'Mind Britain's Business'. While he was an ardent admirer of Hitler – the Führer was guest of honour at his marriage to Diana Mitford in Berlin in 1936 – Mosley exploited a wider desire for peace. His Britain First rally in London's Earls Court Exhibition Hall attracted 30,000 people in July 1939, and he continued to press for a deal with Germany once the war had started. But with the invasion of France and the ascendancy of Winston Churchill in May 1940, there was no more tolerance for British fascism. Mosley was interned without trial under wartime regulations and the BUF was banned.

So why did fascism flop in Britain? We like to tell ourselves flattering stories about our invincible national tolerance and good nature, but it's all nonsense. If the country had been successfully invaded, or simply signed a peace deal with Germany, Britain would have discovered its inner fascist soon enough. Paranoia about Jews, communists and the urban masses was mainstream among the middle and upper classes, snaking through popular fiction. A mystical obsession with the English countryside and Arthurian legend might have nourished home-grown fascism. Figures as prominent as Churchill and D. H. Lawrence had expressed an interest in the biological elitism of eugenics.

The reasons for failure were more pragmatic. While it wasn't spared economic and political crises, as a victorious imperial power Britain never approached the same desperate state as Italy and Germany. The winner-takes-all electoral system denied fascists a foothold in Parliament and a role in a coalition government. Finally, Mosley's overt Nazi sympathies and street violence toxified the party and alienated his powerful supporters. His biggest blunder was to allow his movement to appear exotic and foreign-inspired instead of building a distinctly British brand of fascism. Fascism only ever really succeeds when it presents itself as part of national continuity.

George Orwell witnessed Mosley address a crowd in Barnsley in March 1936 and thought his rhetoric 'unutterable bollox'. But he wrote in *The Road to Wigan Pier* that somebody else might succeed where Mosley had failed: 'When I speak of Fascism in England, I am not necessarily thinking of Mosley and his pimpled followers. English Fascism, when it arrives, is likely to be of a sedate and subtle kind (presumably, at any rate at first, it won't be called Fascism) . . . But what I am thinking of at this moment is the Fascist attitude of mind, which beyond any doubt is gaining ground among people who ought to know better.'

After Mussolini took power in 1922, many American journalists perceived an obvious home-grown precedent. 'Has it occurred to you,' asked a columnist in the *Washington Times*, 'that our American Fascisti are the gentlemen of the Ku Klux Klan?' The Klan themselves hoped that Mussolini would 'join with us in establishing the klan in Italy'.

The Klan arose after the American Civil War and was relaunched in 1915, inspired by the racist propaganda of D. W. Griffith's movie *The Birth of a Nation*. It had mystical rituals (its leader was the Grand Wizard), uniforms (white hoods) and a campaign of guerrilla violence against perceived enemies (primarily black people but also, in its second iteration, immigrants, communists, Catholics and Jews). At its 1920s peak, the Klan's membership was as high as four million. They pitched themselves as 'One Hundred Per Cent Americans' who put 'America First'.

During the Great Depression and the unfolding backlash to Roosevelt's New Deal, the Klan were joined by dozens of fascist or fascist-inspired groups, including the black-shirted American Fascisti, the KKK splinter group the Black Legion,

William Pelley's Silver Legion of America, and the Christian Front, founded by the viciously antisemitic Catholic radio host Father Charles Coughlin. The celebrity aviator Charles Lindbergh gained considerable influence as a pro-Nazi appeaser who offered a version of Oswald Mosley's 'peace fascism' under the banner of 'America First'. Dorothy Thompson, who had covered European fascism since the beginning and held the proud distinction of being the first American journalist to have been expelled from Germany by the Nazis, summed up American fascism's base: 'The dispossessed and humiliated of the middle classes, bankrupt farmers, cracker-box radicals, and the "respectable" but extremely discontented provincials.'

The strongest of them all was the explicitly pro-Nazi German-American Bund, which packed out New York's Madison Square Garden as late as February 1939. The Bund added the swastika to the American eagle, just as the Imperial Fascist League had planted it in the middle of the Union Jack. But this obvious foreign influence doomed them, and all the rest, just as it had sunk Mosley.

'When and if fascism comes to America,' said the Yale professor Halford E. Luccock in 1938, echoing Orwell, 'it will not be labelled "made in Germany"; it will not be marked with a swastika; it will not even be called fascism; it will be called, of course, "Americanism".' One figure of concern, until his assassination in 1935, had been the demagogic Louisiana governor Huey Long. 'American Fascism would never emerge as a Fascist but as a 100 per cent American movement,' Long told Thompson. Thompson's husband, Sinclair Lewis, satirised Long as the oafish dictator Buzz Windrip in his novel *It Can't Happen Here*. The implication of the title was of course that it *could* happen here.

Fascist and proto-fascist ideas, after all, were mainstream in the US. Two bestselling books – Madison Grant's *The Passing of the Great Race* (1916) and Lothrop Stoddard's *The Rising Tide of Color: The Threat Against White World-Supremacy* (1920) – advocated eugenics and white supremacy. Hitler was significantly inspired by their work. He hailed Grant's book as his 'Bible' and plagiarised passages from it in *Mein Kampf*. As late as 1940, Stoddard visited Nazi Germany and complained that its eugenics policies, which were explicitly modelled on America's, did not go far enough.

Far more authoritarian than their British counterparts, who kept eugenics off the statute books, American eugenicists were instrumental in drawing up the racist, antisemitic 1924 Immigration Act, which later prevented many Jewish refugees from escaping Europe, including the family of Anne Frank. President Calvin Coolidge was a eugenicist, too. 'The Nordics propagate themselves successfully,' he wrote. 'With other races, the outcome shows deterioration on both sides.'

Black writers on fascism have argued that many core US policies were effectively fascist. The poet Langston Hughes described slavery, segregation and the genocide of Native Americans as 'our native fascisms'. In principle, liberal democracies and fascism are irreconcilable. In practice, they sometimes have shared methods and goals.

In her mischievous 1941 essay 'Who Goes Nazi?', Thompson wrote about the 'somewhat macabre parlour game' of guessing which of one's acquaintances might embrace fascism under the right circumstances: the anti-feminist, the antisemitic populist, the spoilt narcissist, the bitter social climber. 'Nazism has nothing to do with race and nationality,' she wrote. 'It appeals to a certain type of mind.'

FASCISM

*

The interwar period was an era of dictators in Europe, but only two of them were avowed fascists. In fact, dictators made the most effective anti-fascists. They sometimes co-opted the insurgent energy of fascist movements, but once those movements became too radical and ambitious, they were neutered or suppressed.

Greece, Portugal, Poland and Lithuania all experienced military coups during the 1920s, shutting the door to fascism. António Salazar, Portugal's dictator between 1932 and 1968, provided a pretty good definition of fascism when he rejected the 'exaltation of youth, the cult of force through so-called direct action, the principle of the superiority of state political power in social life, the propensity for organising masses behind a single leader'. The Greek dictator Ioannis Metaxas explicitly compared his regime to 'Portugal under Dr Salazar, not the Germany of Hitler or the Italy of Mussolini'.

Fascism made the greatest advances in three relatively young nations, destabilised by war and economic crisis, riven by divisions, prone to nationalism and antisemitism, and paranoid about communism: Austria, Romania and Hungary. Austria's Nazi Party was making significant headway until 1934, when it murdered chancellor Engelbert Dollfuss and was brutally suppressed by his successor, Kurt Schuschnigg.

In Hungary, the fascistic nationalist Gyula Gömbös was assimilated and muzzled by the authoritarian military leader Miklós Horthy. Appointed prime minister in 1932 on the condition that he renounce antisemitism, Gömbös spoke of introducing fascist policies, but when he died suddenly in 1936, his plan died with him. When Hungarian fascism rose again with the National Socialist Arrow Cross, which claimed 250,000 members by 1939, Horthy did not allow it the democratic space to become a serious threat. Only in 1944, when Hitler soured on Horthy and invaded Hungary, did the Arrow Cross leader, Ferenc Szálasi, become prime minister (for three months) and deport Hungary's Jews to the death camps. Across Europe, fascists could only enter government if Hitler put them there. Like Vidkun Quisling's National Government in Norway or Ante Pavelić's genocidal Ustaše in Croatia, Szálasi's was a puppet regime.

The strangest and most startling form of fascism arose in Romania. The Legion of the Archangel Michael (also known as the Iron Guard) was somewhere between a fascist movement and a religious sect. Its handsome, theatrical leader Corneliu Zelea Codreanu was a nationalist mystic who promised Romania a 'spiritual resurrection'. He had become famous at the age of 25 after he was acquitted of murdering a senior police officer (the jurors wore swastikas), and gained influence during the Great Depression. He was frothingly antisemitic, enthusiastically pro-Nazi and somewhat mad.

Like the Arrow Cross, the Legion boasted a quarter of a million members. But Codreanu was too fanatical to be co-opted, so in 1938, the authoritarian regime of King Carol II had him arrested, garrotted and shot. After Carol's abdication in 1940, General Ion Antonescu brought the Legion into his dictatorship, with Hitler's blessing, and proclaimed Romania a National Legionary State, but he soon grew impatient with its horrendous antisemitic violence. When it attempted a coup in January 1941, he wiped it out.

In all of these cases, the significant distinction was not moral. Authoritarian dictators shared many of the fascists' prejudices and hatreds. But the movement's revolutionary fervour was threatening to them. They wanted to control a sedate, passive populace and were not in the business of whipping it up into a state of violent excitement about racial destiny.

Fascism was a European phenomenon with imitators around the world. In South Africa, fascist-inspired groups helped to push the National Party towards the establishment of the racist apartheid system. In Asia, there were fascist-inspired nationalist movements in India (the RSS) and China (the Blue Shirts Society). In the Middle East, Syria, Iraq and Egypt all saw significant fascist movements. Mussolini and Hitler actively supported Arab nationalists such as the violently antisemitic Palestinian Amin al-Husseini, Grand Mufti of Jerusalem. There was even a fascist splinter of Zionism called Brit HaBirionim (the Strongmen Alliance). In Latin America, so-called 'shirt movements' sprang up in Brazil, Bolivia, Chile, Mexico and Peru. But it was a familiar story: they were either crushed by conservative dictators (Brazil's Integralists) or diluted their ambitions in order to gain power (Bolivia's Movimiento Nacionalista Revolucionario).

Everywhere fascism was attempted outside Italy and Germany it failed in one way or another. But plenty of right-wing dictators did succeed. Perhaps they were fascists at heart?

It is often argued that the long-lasting dictatorships of Spain's General Franco and Portugal's António Salazar were fascist in practice if not in principle. During the Spanish Civil War, anyone fighting for the Republic would have said they were fighting fascism. Were they right?

Francisco Franco's path to power could not have been more different from Hitler and Mussolini's. He was not a working-class outsider but a career soldier from an upper-class Catholic military family that had produced six generations of naval officers. A war hero in North Africa, he became, at 33, the youngest general in Europe. He had no political journey to speak of: his values were essentially those of his parents. He was a conservative monarchist with no interest in socialism of any kind. He neither built a movement from scratch nor contested elections. He achieved supremacy at the age of 46 by leading a successful military revolt, rather than through a combination of street violence and political chicanery. The Spanish Civil War would have happened with or without him; he just schemed his way to the front of the coup.

So how fascist was Franco's regime? That depends on your definition. He certainly mimicked fascism's rituals: the Roman salute, the military parades, the ritual chants. He anointed himself *Caudillo*, the Spanish equivalent of *Duce* or *Führer*, at the head of a one-party state. He even built a cult of personality despite having, in the words of Samuel Hoare, Britain's ambassador to Spain, all the magnetism of 'a doctor with a big family practice and an assured income'.

With his lifelong paranoia about a 'Jewish-Masonic-Bolshevik conspiracy', Franco claimed that his coup was necessary to save the Spanish people from degeneration. His propagandist, Ernesto Giménez Caballero, alarmingly described him as 'the phallus that will penetrate Spain . . . to the point that it is impossible to know whether Spain is Franco or Franco is Spain'.

Franco repressed his enemies with brutal zeal, delaying victory in the civil war so as to obliterate the Republicans rather than merely defeat them. He called this 'the moral redemption of the occupied zones'. His 'White Terror' killed 200,000 people during the war and around 20,000 during his first few years in power. Some half a million supporters of the Republic left Spain to avoid persecution, including the surrealist artists Pablo Picasso and Luis Buñuel. Franco was considerably more dangerous to his own people than Mussolini was to his, treating the Spanish working classes like the colonial subjects he had slaughtered in Morocco earlier in his career.

In many ways, then, Franco was indistinguishable from fascism. Certainly to anyone victimised by his regime the distinction would have been academic. But as always, the differences are as important as the similarities. Franco craved order and stability, rather than the volatile enthusiasm of the fascists, who he absorbed and marginalised. His regime rested on the traditional conservative pillars of army, business, church and state, not the party. In fact, his personal power exceeded that of Hitler and Mussolini because he ruled by decree without even the pretence of cabinet or parliament, and gave his party no say in government. His militant Catholicism left no space for the 'civic religion' of fascism and his conservatism did not require building a totalitarian parallel structure. Nor was he interested in creating a fascist New Man.

The extent of the difference between Franco and Mussolini can be seen in how the Caudillo treated Spain's actual fascist party, the Falange Española de las Juntas de Ofensiva Nacional Sindicalista. Co-founded in 1934 by José Antonio Primo de Rivera, whose father, Miguel, had been Spain's shallow, impetuous military dictator between 1923 and 1930, it fashioned a muddle of competing interests into an Italian-style fascist party with a programme called the 27 Points. Primo de Rivera described the Falange Española as 'a movement and not a party – indeed, you could almost call it an anti-party . . . neither of the Right nor of the Left'. Those words could have been spoken by Mussolini.

But the Falange won just 0.7 per cent of the vote in the

February 1936 general election, and its blue-shirted thugs fared badly in street battles against equally ferocious leftists. Only the Spanish Civil War saved the Falangists from oblivion. Rallying behind the coup, they saw their numbers balloon a hundredfold. But three in five of the party's pre-war membership died in the war, including Primo de Rivera, which made it a much less militant organisation. In April 1937, Franco merged the party with the Catholic conservative party Comunión Tradicionalista to form the Falange Española Tradicionalista y de las Juntas de Ofensiva Nacional Sindicalista – the basis of a one-party state. Although he embraced 26 of the Falange's 27 Points, they were all disposable. Fascism was subsumed into Francoism.

Crucially, Franco's only ambition was to rule Spain; he was not obsessed with territorial expansion through war. Despite his military debt to Italy and Germany and his involvement in their Anti-Comintern Pact, he kept his distance and rebuffed efforts to bring Spain into the Second World War because its war-ravaged economy was not remotely ready for another great conflict. Hitler said that he would rather have his teeth pulled out than negotiate with that 'Jesuit swine' ever again. Once the tide of the war turned against the fascist regimes, Franco banned the Roman salute and other fascist paraphernalia.

Authoritarianism is far more effective at exercising power over the long term than fascism. It is in the business of running marathons, not sprints. It does not burn itself out in a frenzy of perpetual movement. If fascism was dynamic, then Franco was content to be static. He died in bed on 20 November 1975 at the age of 82, having outlived Hitler and Mussolini by 30 years.

Anti-fascist writers such as Joseph Roth, Karel Čapek and Albert Camus compared fascism to a pathogen that should have been quarantined while there was still time. At the end of Camus's allegorical 1947 novel *The Plague*, a doctor warns that 'the plague bacillus never dies or disappears for good'. It lies dormant and bides its time until it can 'rouse up its rats again and send them forth to die in a happy city'. Many post-war writers were obsessed with understanding how fascism had happened and how it might one day return.

During the Cold War, fascism was largely neutralised in Europe. Behind the Iron Curtain, it was suppressed. In the West, it made little headway, even during the economic crises of the 1970s. On the one hand, overtly fascist groups were no more than cranks and terrorists. On the other, fascist-inspired political parties such as the Movimento Sociale Italiano had to moderate their message in order to attract voters. Parties that attempted to fuse parliamentary and paramilitary tactics, like the UK's National Front, soon lost momentum.

Across much of the world, however, the machinations of the superpowers and the chaotic end of empire produced a new era of dictators. Part of the reason that the study of fascism is so vast and contentious is because the world has seen several authoritarians who resemble Hitler and Mussolini without actually calling themselves fascists. Is fascism what you say you are or what you do?

One hotly debated case is Juan Domingo Perón's regime in Argentina. The country had the most established radical-right tradition in South America, going back to the 1900s, and a pro-fascist military dictatorship from 1943 to 1946. A former military attaché in Mussolini's Italy, Perón said that 'Mussolini was the greatest man of our century, but he committed certain disastrous errors.' Between 1946 and 1955, Perón ruled as an authoritarian, with his glamorous wife Eva Perón (later the unlikely subject of an Andrew Lloyd Webber musical) significantly boosting his appeal. Opponents were censored, arrested and tortured, starting in the universities. 'Build the Fatherland. Kill a student,' ran one slogan. Prominent Nazi war criminals were offered a safe haven. The historian Paul M. Hayes has called Perónism 'a form of fascism that was distinctively Latin American', but others prefer to label Perón a magpie pragmatist. Certainly by fascist standards his ambitions were modest and his powers sufficiently limited that he could eventually be ousted by a military coup.

The late-twentieth-century dictatorships of General Augusto Pinochet in Chile, General Leopoldo Galtieri in Argentina, Muʾammar Gaddafi in Libya and Saddam Hussein in Iraq were by no means the same phenomenon, but they all featured some combination of extreme nationalism, militarism, strongman leaders, one-party rule, contempt for democracy, suppression of liberties, persecution of 'enemies within' and enormous violence.

The case of Saddam Hussein is the most extreme. Founded in the 1940s, the Ba'ath Party (the name means 'renaissance') combined revolutionary non-Marxist socialism with Arab nationalism, fuelled by mythic notions of racial superiority and regeneration. Legends of past greatness would inspire a New Man. Saddam didn't identify as a fascist, but between 1979 and 2003, his one-party police state had many fascist characteristics: a cult of personality, wars of conquest against Iran and Kuwait, the attempted genocide of the Kurds and the Marsh Arabs, and executions, purges and torture chambers on an immense scale. His secret police 'disappeared' as many as a quarter of a million alleged opponents. Saddam himself closely studied both Hitler and Stalin as examples of 'the successful organization of an entire society by the state for the achievement of national goals'. Stanley G. Payne, whose definition of fascism was relatively strict, argued: 'There will probably never again be a reproduction of the Third Reich, but Saddam Hussein has come closer than any other dictator since 1945.'

And yet it was in Eastern Europe, after the end of the Cold War, that questions about modern fascism had the greatest bearing.

The federal state of Yugoslavia began to lose its legitimacy after the death of President Josip Broz Tito in 1980, with dominant member Serbia struggling to retain control over its other constituent republics. After becoming president of Serbia in 1989, Slobodan Milošević governed as an agitating nationalist whose rhetoric combined historic grievance with extreme aggression against Croatia and Bosnia.

Milošević's efforts to maximise Serbian control within the federation prompted other nationalities to try and separate. In 1991, Slovenia and Croatia declared independence, leading Serb-dominated districts to secede from Croatia with the support of the army. Serbs and Croats both attempted to expel each other through tactics like murder and gang rape. Bosnia's declaration of independence in 1992 was even more painful, given the heavily intermingled communities in which the violence took place. Friends and families who had lived together happily for decades were suddenly engulfed by group violence triggered by incendiary rhetoric. Milošević's attempt to bring Serb-dominated areas of Croatia and Bosnia into a Greater Serbia, and then to expel ethnic Albanians from the province of Kosovo, ultimately failed following Western military interventions, and his rule ended in electoral defeat in 2000. Some 140,000 people had been killed and four million displaced.

What took place in Yugoslavia was not a race war. It was based on historic, cultural and religious group distinctions. Nor was Milošević's regime internally fascist. He was an autocrat, not a dictator. But events nevertheless had a grim resonance with the behaviour of the Nazis. For the first time since the Second World War, Europe witnessed the murder of men, women and children in a territorial war, driven by a narrative of group victimhood and decline. As the scholar Robert O. Paxton wrote: 'While pinning the epithet of *fascist* upon the odious Milosevic adds nothing to an explanation of how his rule was established and maintained, it seems appropriate to recognise a functional equivalent when it appears.'

Meanwhile, in the former USSR, something very closely akin to fascism was also beginning to take hold.

Vladimir Putin was born in October 1952, six months before Stalin died. As a KGB officer, he was a loyal servant of the Soviet Union for many years before the state disintegrated. But once he became prime minister of Russia in August 1999, and president four months later, he took from the Soviets those elements that were unrelated to communism – the characteristics that Stalin shared with Hitler.

Putin ostensibly opposed fascism while acting very much like a fascist. This bait-and-switch has a long tradition in Russia. Stalin was the first person to popularise the use of 'fascist' as an all-purpose insult (in 1924 he called social democracy 'objectively the moderate wing of fascism'), only to ally himself with Hitler in 1939. Yet this pact did not prevent Russia from crafting its subsequent war with Nazi Germany, at the cost of 8.7 million military and 19 million civilian lives, into a national myth of heroic resistance to the evils of fascism. The Russian definition of fascism was simple: it meant anti-Russian. 'Under Stalin,' wrote Timothy Snyder, 'fascism was first indifferent, then it was bad, then it was fine until . . . it was bad again. But no one ever defined what it meant. It was a box into which anything could be put . . . Because Soviet anti-fascism just meant defining an enemy, it offered fascism a backdoor through which to return to Russia.'

The most important obsession that Putin borrowed from Stalinism was nationalism. Aware that his Georgian origins inspired suspicion and derision, Stalin had turned himself into an aggressive Russian nationalist, killing 250,000 members of ethnic minorities for alleged treason. When Soviet communism collapsed between 1989 and 1991, Russia lost not only its satellite states in Eastern Europe and the Baltic but partners such as Ukraine and Georgia. Russia's transition to democracy and capitalism in the 1990s was so abrupt and badly managed that it caused immense chaos and suffering, enriching a new elite of ruthless oligarchs at the expense of ordinary citizens. Many Russians came to feel that, rather than voluntarily dismantling a dictatorship, they had been defeated, albeit not in battle. This produced a burning sense of humiliation and resentment similar to that which the losers of the First World War had felt. Putin offered to remedy that.

Like Milošević, whose national mythology of Serb victimhood wound back absurdly far to the Battle of Kosovo between Serbia and the Ottoman Empire in 1389, Putin rooted his nationalism in the centuries before communism. His narrative of stolen glory invoked not just Stalin but Peter the Great, the first Emperor and Autocrat of All the Russias. He waged a seven-year war with separatists in the Russian republic of Chechnya and a five-day one against Georgia over the disputed region of South Ossetia. The initial attack on Chechnya in 1999, in response to alleged terrorist atrocities, was the event that transformed Putin from a grey, anonymous bureaucrat into a popular national leader.

Around the time he retook the presidency in 2012, Putin gave up on seeking the approval of the international community and fully embraced Russian nationalism. He introduced new laws to suppress opposition, in the name of fighting extremism, blasphemy, treason and 'foreign influence'. He began to demonise NATO and the European Union and sought to make Russia the heart of its own Eurasian empire. If Russia could not become stronger, it would make the West weaker.

Putin regarded Ukraine, especially its Russian-speaking eastern regions, the same way that Hitler had viewed Alsace–Lorraine or Mussolini had seen Fiume: as territory that had been stolen or given away and needed to be reabsorbed, with the superficial justification of protecting Russian-speakers from their wicked oppressors. The myth of Russian innocence was fundamental to him: a nation besieged, undermined and tormented. He blamed Ukraine's popular revolt against Russian influence in 2014 on 'nationalists, neo-Nazis, Russophobes and antisemites'. In response, he annexed Crimea and installed puppet governments in Russian-speaking Donetsk and Luhansk, lighting the fuse for a full-scale invasion of Ukraine in 2022.

At home, too, he has drawn on the more fascistic components of Soviet totalitarianism. Russia still holds elections, but they are pure theatre. Putin controls the media – whose propaganda is disseminated around the world – and dispenses with rivals and opponents, from journalists to oligarchs. Like his fascist predecessors, he sees himself as a man of destiny who embodies the will of his people. Ridiculing his aggressively macho posturing is easy, and fun, but his style has proved successful with his intended audience.

Putin is intellectually indebted to Russian fascism. He has long admired the work of the late Ivan Ilyin, an ultra-nationalist White Russian exile who had dreamt of a Russian equivalent to Hitler and Mussolini and despised the individual: 'Evil begins where the person begins.' In 2006, Putin purchased Ilyin's archive and personally paid for a new tombstone for him in Moscow. The intellectual engine room of the new Russian nationalism was a think-tank called the Izborsk Club, whose manifesto called for a militarised, crusading nation: 'Russia does not need hasty political reform. It needs arms factories and altars.'. Its founder, Alexander Prokhanov, said that antisemitism was 'a result of the fact that Jews took over the world, are using their power for evil', and anticipated replacing the EU with a 'constellation of European fascist states'. Another member, Alexsandr Dugin, declared that the next Russian Revolution would be 'fascism – borderless as our lands, and red as our blood', and promised that it would be a purer, more successful version than that of Hitler or Mussolini. By 2007, he saw fit to declare: 'Putin is everywhere, Putin is everything, Putin is absolute, and Putin is indispensable.'

During the 2010s, the Russian leader's role as the global figurehead of authoritarianism and nationalism became disturbingly apparent. While the mutually suspicious nationalists of the 1920s and 1930s had failed to develop an international fascist network, their twenty-first-century descendants were much more willing to build alliances based on common values and shared enemies. And Putin would stand at the centre of this network.

CHAPTER SIX
Fascism Today

Around the year 2010, politics began to change. A new kind of politician emerged, or rather a new kind of politician showed they could win. It heralded the era of the populist: the flamboyant, blunt-speaking provocateur and agitator. They rose to prominence around the world, in small countries and large, influential states and obscure ones. No nation was immune.

In some countries, like Poland, Hungary and Italy, populist parties took over the government entirely. In others, like Austria, Bulgaria and Slovakia, they served as junior partners in a governing coalition. In a few, like the US and the UK, populist ideas were absorbed by the traditional centre-right party and inserted into government that way. Even countries that had formerly prided themselves on rejecting this kind of politics, like Germany, Sweden, Portugal and the Netherlands, proved vulnerable.

Populism has a pretty rudimentary founding proposition, which is more akin to a children's story than a political theory. It states that society can be split into two groups: the people and the elite. The people are pure and authentic; the elite are corrupt. The people are the goodies, basically, and the elite are the baddies. Quite who fits into each category changes according to the individual circumstances. For right-wing populists, 'the people' generally refers to the dominant ethnic culture and 'the elite' is composed of liberals and immigrants.

Across the world, populist parties reflect highly distinct regional identities. In India, BJP leader Narendra Modi came from the nationalist Hindutva movement. In Israel, Likud leader Benjamin Netanyahu grounded himself in the hardline tradition of revisionist Zionism. In Brazil, Jair Bolsonaro attracted the support of right-wing Christian evangelicals. The Alternative for Germany party set itself against Muslims, immigrants and the European Union. But whatever their religious or cultural differences, all deployed strikingly similar rhetoric and ideas.

There are some left-wing populists – Nicolás Maduro's regime in Venezuela also trades in a people-versus-the-elite narrative – but the vast majority of successful populist movements emerged as an evolution of far-right thought during the second half of the twentieth century.

During the post-war years, most far-right parties in Europe jettisoned the most toxic elements of fascism: totalitarianism and dictatorship. They embraced, in words if not in action, democracy and liberty. Starting with the New Right in France in the 1960s and 1970s, they also rejected explicit racism for a more subtle concept called 'ethnopluralism'. This argued that ethnic groups were not necessarily superior or inferior to one another, but that they nevertheless remained distinct. Humans were ill-suited to living alongside different cultures. Multiculturalism was therefore a crime against the human condition. This was the main argument for nativism: the belief that states should be populated exclusively by members of the native group.

In practice, racism was never far from the surface. Language about foreign nationals was incessantly hostile and negative, particularly regarding the threat of crime or sexual assault, which was often treated as an exclusively immigrant phenomenon. But ethnopluralism allowed the far right to deracialise its rhetoric. Now it could speak about 'culture' rather than 'race', earning it a place in respectable political discourse.

These ideas were buttressed by a new conspiracy theory, which bore a striking resemblance to *The Protocols of the Elders of Zion*, the early-twentieth-century hoax that purported to reveal a secret Jewish plan for world domination. It was called the Great Replacement theory. Popularised by the French far-right writers Jean Raspail and Renaud Camus, it held that immigration was not the result of people fleeing poverty or turmoil to find new opportunities in the West, but instead a secret plan orchestrated by progressive politicians to undermine their own nations, or simply replace their white working-class voters. George Soros, a wealthy Hungarian hedge fund manager and philanthropist who funded liberal projects across the world, was often portrayed as the evil genius behind it, a kind of Cobra Commander pulling the strings of the progressive conspiracy. The fact that he was Jewish, his critics insisted unconvincingly, was just an unfortunate coincidence.

Three events took place in the early years of the twenty-first century that gave these ideas a dramatic boost. The first was the terrorist attack on New York and Washington DC on 11 September 2001, which fuelled a narrative about Muslims being a direct threat to Western civilisation, much like European Jews a century earlier. The second was the financial crash of 2008, which produced in many countries a bruising period of austerity and reduced living standards. This benefited the far right, much as hyperinflation and the Great Depression had boosted Hitler. The third event was the refugee crisis in 2015, when asylum seekers, predominantly fleeing the war in Syria, made their way to Europe in relatively high numbers. Taken together, the events provided a version of the conditions that made early-twentieth-century Europe vulnerable to fascism: a perceived foreign threat, a decline in material conditions, and a frustration with the supposed impotence of ruling political parties.

The subsequent rise in support for European populist parties was meteoric. In France in 2002, for example, the National Front's Jean-Marie Le Pen made it to the presidential run-off with 16.9 per cent of the vote, triggering a spasm of outrage and shock. A surge in turnout in the second round managed to hold the far-right leader at 17.8 per cent. But 15 years later, Le Pen's daughter, Marine, won 33.9 per cent in the second round. There was much less outrage this time, and no shock. Her strong performance was considered par for the populist course. That same year, Alternative for Germany became the first hard-right party to win seats in the German parliament since the Nazis. In 2022, Le Pen secured 41.5 per cent in the second round. In 2024, Le Pen's party was only denied victory in the parliamentary elections by a last-minute alliance of centrists and a left-wing Popular Front, reminiscent of 1936.

We now live in an era of populist politics. In nearly every single Western democracy, populist parties vie for supremacy with traditional parties on the centre right or left. There is as a result a fierce debate about whether populism is fascism, either in general or in specific cases.

Perhaps the biggest obstacle to understanding fascism is the simple fact that every schoolchild learns far more about

Nazi Germany than any other authoritarian regime. Hitler therefore becomes synonymous with dictator, Goebbels with propaganda, the Holocaust with persecution. If you invoke 1930s Germany to criticise a draconian right-wing policy, you will be widely understood. But if, for the sake of accuracy, you reference modern Hungary, 1970s Chile, 1940s Spain, or even 1920s Italy, most people will not have any idea what you are talking about. This narrow band of shared knowledge erases most of the history of authoritarianism and creates a false binary: either a country is a healthy, tolerant democracy or it is on the road to Nazism. The vast middle ground must be understood, now more than ever, because that is where the populists operate. Even if we are in the business of sounding the red alert about them, we must have a sense of the precise threat they pose if we are to effectively challenge them.

As always, there are in fact two parallel debates taking place. The first is a historical discussion about whether populist parties bear enough of a resemblance to Mussolini or Hitler to be validly described as fascists. In certain areas, like their acceptance of democratic elections, they plainly do not. But in others, like the adoption of conspiracy theories to target minorities, or their hatred of Marxism, they contain an echo of what has come before. Fascism and populism share a conceptual root. They both feature an all-encompassing insistence on the 'will of the people' as the only source of political legitimacy, unlike liberalism, which places a strong emphasis on individual rights, diversity and the separation of powers.

The second debate is about urgency. When is it time to pull the emergency alarm marked 'fascism'? When is it suitable to summon memories of Nazi evil, so that people can recognise the danger of these new forces on the right? This alarm has, of course, been rendered less effective by decades of left-wingers wrongly using the word to brand figures like George W. Bush and Tony Blair. But that does not invalidate its use now. Perhaps certain populists are demonstrating a sufficient level of extremism and proximity to power that the word needs to be used, even if only to shock people out of their complacency. As Primo Levi wrote: 'Every age has its own fascism.'

Sometimes these two debates directly address one another. Giorgia Meloni, for instance, became prime minister of Italy in 2022. As a teenager she had been an activist for the Movimento Sociale Italiano, the explicitly fascist group that was established in 1946 by veterans of Mussolini's Republic of Salò. In power, though, she proved a far more moderate figure than many of her fellow populist leaders, forming effective working relationships with figures like European Commission president Ursula von der Leyen and centre-left German chancellor Olaf Scholz. Meloni's example demonstrates that even direct lineage to fascist parties is not a firm indicator of fascist tendencies. The reality is far more complex and unpredictable.

There are two essential examples of the populist wave. The first is Hungary's Viktor Orbán, who is arguably the most explicit champion of the cause; the second is America's Donald Trump, whose behaviour in the world's most powerful country serves as an inspiration for populists everywhere.

Orbán came to power as the leader of the Fidesz party in 2010, after the financial crash had pulverised Hungary's economy. His rhetoric on race and ethnicity was always disturbing but became more extreme as the years wore on. 'The alteration of a country's ethnic makeup amounts to an alteration of its cultural identity,' he said in 2017. In 2022, he made a speech in Romania: 'This is why we have always fought: we are willing to mix with one another, but we do not want to become peoples of mixed-race.' Hungary, he said, would not join Western Europe's 'mixed-race world'.

This is a classic example of the cynical euphemistic game played by ethnopluralism. The word 'race' generally stays off the table, or is downplayed. It's too explosive. 'Culture' and 'ethnicity' take its place. Indeed, in a press conference shortly after the Romania speech, Orbán insisted that it 'is not a race issue for us, this is a cultural issue'. But the very notion of ethnic homogeneity captures the assumptions shared by Nazism and Orbánism. Unlike liberalism, which sees society as composed of individuals with individual rights, Orbán prioritises an unvarying ethnic category that defines its culture and political leadership. Any minority rights that do not correspond to the 'will of the people' are therefore an irrelevance. So while he does not talk explicitly about racial supremacy, he participates in precisely the kind of rhetoric that formed the basis of fascism's appeal and contributed to its worst excesses.

This message is compounded by the manner in which Fidesz speaks about immigrants, particularly Muslims. A typical image, reproduced with regularity in government-controlled tabloids like *Lokal*, is of an attractive white woman next to the pixelated image of a dark-skinned man who has just assaulted her. Refugees are often described as uncivilised or subhuman. As Zsolt Bayer, a ring-wing commentator and founder member of Fidesz, said in 2017: 'This barbaric herd, which should be eliminated, raped women in Milan again. Will they stay in Europe, what do you guys think?'

Muslims compose only 0.4 per cent of Hungary's

population, but government propaganda has created wide-spread support for conspiracy theories that are remarkably similar to those spread by Hitler about Jews. A 2018 poll by the think-tank Political Capital found that 45 per cent of Hungarians believed Muslim leaders had a secret plan to conquer Europe, 48 per cent believed Muslims intended to force their culture on Hungary by stealth, and 51 per cent agreed that Soros was the driving force behind the process.

In a strange dance of antisemitism and Islamophobia, Orbán portrays Soros in a manner that is basically inter-changeable with early-twentieth-century fascist rhetoric against Jews. 'We are fighting an enemy that is different from us,' he said. 'Not open but hiding; not straightforward but crafty; not honest but base; not national but international; does not believe in working but speculates with money; does not have its own homeland but feels it owns the whole world.'

This kind of discourse has created vicious bursts of hatred. A 2017 'national consultation' over an entirely imagined plan by Soros to introduce free immigration to Hungary saw billboards depicting the financier with the words: 'Don't let Soros have the last laugh!' Some were defaced with graffiti reading: 'Stinking Jew'. A Fidesz MP posted a photo of a dead pig on Facebook with the phrase: 'This was Soros.' Eventually, Soros's Open Society Foundations closed its offices in Buda-pest, saying that it was 'impossible to protect the security of our operations and our staff in Hungary'. Hungary has not experienced a Kristallnacht. But the language, and the reaction to it, bear comparison.

The same jumble of similarities and differences can be seen in the attempt to control society. In modern Hungary, there is barely any interference with private life at all. Orbán has no interest in the soul of the citizen. There is, however, a significant form of authoritarian societal control, which gives the regime dominion over public discourse. During Fidesz's time in power, parliament, the press, the courts and civil society have been steadily taken over by party loyalists, until barely any independent voices are left at all.

The party started buying up media outlets in the 1990s. This followed a set pattern. They would purchase a publishing house or TV station, either directly or through a network of oligarchs, force it to adopt a strictly pro-Fidesz position, then boost its finances with advertising from other business interests. This was the tactic deployed with *Magyar Nemzet*, the largest daily paper, and Hír TV, Hungary's first TV news channel.

By 2018, all subtlety was gone. The oligarchs donated 476 media outlets to a new government-run body, the Central European Press and Media Foundation, giving Orbán direct control over the country's major media assets: cable news, internet sites, tabloid newspapers, sports papers, regional press, lifestyle magazines, radio stations.

The judiciary, meanwhile, was neutralised. A new constitution passed by Fidesz prevented the constitutional court from overruling anything voted on by parliament. A new National Judicial Office was given power over judicial appointments, allowing it to purge the courts of anyone who could stand up to Orbán.

The attack extended to civil society. The Hungarian Academy of Sciences was brought under state control, as was the much-respected historical 1956 Institute. A new body called the Klebelsberg Institution Maintenance Centre was given authority over primary and secondary schools. It ensured that every headteacher was a Fidesz loyalist. This led to changes in the curriculum, with one textbook reading: 'It can be problematic for different cultures to coexist.' Government-appointed figures were installed at the head of the opera and literary museums. Even the position of editor of a cooking magazine was reserved for a Fidesz loyalist.

Orbán, like other populists, claims to be a supporter of democracy – albeit, in his words, 'illiberal democracy'. But his commitment is extremely superficial. In practice, measures have been taken to stack the odds heavily in favour of Fidesz. The number of members of parliament was reduced to ensure Fidesz control. Constituency boundaries were redrawn to be more favourable to Fidesz-leaning rural voters. Full voting rights were handed to the Hungarian diaspora in countries like Romania, Slovakia, Serbia and Ukraine, in such a way as to maximise the Fidesz vote. And most importantly, Orbán's complete control over the media means the opposition has little chance to make its voice heard.

As we've seen, far more authoritarian dictatorships, like that of Franco in Spain, were not fascist, even though they imposed one-party rule much more comprehensively than Orbán has in Hungary. But there is something deeply disturbing about this combination of factors: the dismantling of meaningful democracy, the agitation of the populace against minorities, and the demand for ethnic homogeneity. Taken one by one, they are clearly well below the fascist threshold. Taken together, they summon the spectres of the past.

Of all the populists, none has inspired more anxious debate about twenty-first-century fascism than US President Donald Trump. Since 2015, numerous historians have published essays with titles such as 'Calling Trump the F-Word', 'How Fascist Is Donald Trump?' and 'American Fascism: It Has Happened

Here'. During Trump's term in office, punchy, urgent books like Jason Stanley's *How Fascism Works* and former Secretary of State Madeleine Albright's *Fascism: A Warning* became bestsellers. The buzzword was 'normalisation': the danger of treating Trump as an unusually obnoxious Republican politician rather than something frighteningly new. Incompetence, indiscipline and the strength of American institutions limited what he could do during his first term, but many of his opponents detected in him a fascist heart.

No other populist has presented such a complex web of ways in which they do and do not deserve the damning moniker. In nearly everything Trump does, there are echoes of fascism. And in nearly every case, there are caveats or qualifiers. After all, fascism is a nebulous, changeable, doctrinally vacuous creation, and Trump is a highly inconsistent bundle of instincts with very strong chaos energy. It is therefore hardly surprising that similarities arise, then disappear, and subsequently re-emerge in mutated form.

Trump is perhaps the best demonstration of the idea that successful fascist movements will not hark back to Mussolini or Hitler but instead ground themselves in their country's own culture and history, like Sinclair Lewis's fictional 1930s demagogue Buzz Windrip. As the US neoconservative Robert Kagan wrote before the 2016 election: 'This is how fascism comes to America, not with jackboots and salutes . . . but with a television huckster.'

Trump's style would, of course, have been inconceivable to Hitler, grounded as it is in the manners and techniques he learned during his time as a reality-TV star. But then Hitler's own oratory was a response to the birth pangs of mass suffrage and mass media. It was a technique designed to rile up and motivate the crowds – a quality traditional conservatives envied, just as many American conservatives now envy Trump's ease in front of the camera.

The culture of leader worship around Trump is different from that around Mussolini or Hitler in a more meaningful way. There is in Trump, as with Orbán, no trace of an interest in the soul. There is no attempt to reach deep into people's consciences and mould a New Man. This is partly down to the American obsession with personal freedom, at least for one's own kind, but it is also the case for all the populists. You do not see this aspect of fascism repeated anywhere. It has been completely dropped. Perhaps it is because it is seen as impossible, or undesirable, or an electoral liability. But whatever the reason, it simply does not exist in the modern era.

What does still apply is a cult of personality. And this functions, by and large, in an almost identical manner to the way it functioned a century ago. Trump's huge campaign rallies have a dark, furious energy that is more similar to Hitler's than to traditional US political campaigning. Like Hitler, Trump keeps the leader–follower bond fresh with a collection of symbols and rituals. During his first presidential campaign, red MAGA hats – meaning 'Make America Great Again' – became ubiquitous. Chants of 'lock her up' – a reference to his Democratic rival Hillary Clinton – rang out repeatedly at these events. When Ronald Reagan and Bill Clinton promised to 'make America great again', it sounded like conventional political boosterism. But Trump's usage plays into his bigger narrative about national degeneracy and rebirth. He likes to talk about America as a disaster that only he can redeem.

Whereas early fascist parties began as extra-parliamentary movements in opposition to a failing establishment, Trump was the legitimate nominee of one of America's two main political parties – a significant distinction. But the rallies showed that he was building a parasitical new movement inside the body of the Republican Party. As opposition from party elites crumbled and fundamental conservative assumptions were demolished, the parasite consumed its host. Soon the Republican Party was MAGA, and MAGA was Trump.

'I could stand in the middle of Fifth Avenue and shoot somebody, and I wouldn't lose any voters, OK?' Trump remarked at a 2016 campaign stop in Iowa. This was probably true. After he reluctantly left office in 2021, court proceedings against him for crimes as disparate as sexual assault and insurrection produced no reduction in the strength of support from his movement, and in fact may have increased it. George Orwell, remember, wrote about the appeal of Hitler's image as 'a man suffering under intolerable wrongs . . . He is the martyr, the victim . . . the self-sacrificing hero who fights single-handed against impossible odds.' Trump similarly weaponised every criticism, prosecution or setback to present himself as simultaneously a strongman and a persecuted underdog battling the system. But the cult of the leader alone is not enough to produce fascism. Left-wing autocrats like Fidel Castro in Cuba and Hugo Chávez in Venezuela have shown that a demagogue is not necessarily a fascist.

Other aspects of Trump's programme follow this trend – inviting comparisons to fascism without necessarily being strong enough to warrant the use of the term. Like Mussolini and Hitler, he sometimes seemed suspicious of capitalist elites, despite being a real-estate tycoon and former host of the dog-eat-dog reality game show *The Apprentice*. 'For too long, a small group in our nation's capital has reaped the rewards of government, while the people have borne the cost,' he said in his 2017 inauguration speech. 'Politicians prospered, but the jobs left and the factories closed.' He was particularly hostile to global free trade and its benefits to China. But in office he showed almost no interest in interfering with business and introduced a conventionally Republican package of massive tax cuts that favoured the wealthy. Instead, like Hitler before him, he translated socioeconomic anxieties into sociocultural narratives.

Populism is not so much a programme for government as the perpetual weaponisation of grievances. Trump's administration was defined by a relentless energy, a kind of sustained chaos, in which multiple policies were often announced in the space of a single day and journalists spent much of their time trying to write up the scandalised reaction to one statement only to find that the outrage had already migrated to the next one. This was a reflection of the frenzied and spasmodic nature of Trump's personality, and his typically demagogic preference for loyal mediocrities over talented officials who might challenge him. But it had a purpose too. As Steve Bannon, his short-lived chief strategist, said, the administration intended to 'flood the zone with shit'. This was presented as a way to bamboozle the media, but it also had echoes of the Nazi need for constant and overwhelming dynamism.

On a policy level, the echoes are there, but there is a distinct danger of confirmation bias – finding matches and then building a picture from them that might not be sustainable if you were taking the situation as a whole. A far more meaningful analysis emerges if we instead focus on what Trump says, and how the things he says translate into concrete political actions. And that's when things become truly sinister. The fascist component of his rhetoric has escalated dramatically since 2021.

Trump's comments on immigrants were originally in the ethnopluralist tradition, but his language became increasingly extreme after he left the White House. Seeking re-election, he began to speak of immigrants as a kind of racial contamination. 'They're poisoning the blood of our country,' he said in December 2023. 'That's what they've done. They poison mental institutions and prisons all over the world.' This was the metaphor Hitler used when he said the 'Teutonic element' in North America had been successful because it kept its 'racial stock pure' and would only stay that way as long as it did 'not fall a victim to the habit of adulterating its blood'.

On 11 November 2023, Trump posted on social media: 'We pledge to you that we will root out the Communists, Marxists, Fascists, and Radical Left Thugs that live like vermin within the confines of our Country, lie, steal, and cheat on Elections, and will do anything possible, whether legally or illegally, to destroy America, and the American Dream. The threat from outside forces is far less sinister, dangerous, and grave, than the threat from within.' If you exclude the word 'fascism' and swap 'America' for 'Germany', every part of that passage could have come directly from Hitler's mouth. To portray political opponents as evildoers to be crushed is antithetical to democracy's project of reconciling competing interests. Since his first campaign, Trump has painted a bleak, dystopian picture of 'American carnage' to fuel a narrative of humiliation and decline leading to rebirth and revenge.

Many of Trump's enemies are largely imaginary. The fascists of the 1920s and 1930s could point to Russia and claim with some legitimacy that they were defending their nations from Bolshevism, but there is precisely zero chance of a communist revolution in present-day America. In its absence, Trump must exaggerate fringe groups (Antifa), academic theses (critical race theory) and nebulous concepts (woke) into un-American existential threats. Even Joe Biden, a veteran centrist Democrat, has been reimagined as a puppet of Marxism. The more powerful and wicked the enemy is made to seem, the greater the justification for a drastic response. 'In 2016, I declared: I am your voice,' Trump told a conservative conference in March 2023. 'Today I add: I am your warrior. I am your justice. And to those wronged and betrayed, I am your vengeance.'

Trump's relationship with violence has a disturbing connection to early fascist thought. It is not that he shares fascism's lust for war – indeed, he is decidedly less interested in military confrontation than any of his recent predecessors. He launched no new interventions and began to wind down existing military involvements. He worked to undermine NATO. This is another distinctly American feature. The long tradition of 'America First' isolationism stretches back to the Ku Klux Klan's suspicion of the League of Nations and Charles Lindbergh's opposition to war against Germany.

But even if Trump was no warmonger, he did incite violence at home – and indeed revelled in it. Like Hitler and Mussolini, he seemed to consider it virtuous and laudable, speaking of police violence against journalists as 'actually a beautiful sight'. He is fundamentally a bully. As the journalist Adam Serwer wrote in a landmark essay: 'The cruelty is the point.'

Trump saw politics itself as a form of warfare between irreconcilable factions rather than a democratic contest. The refrain 'lock her up', which acted as both a battle cry and a collective celebration during early Trump rallies, was ostensibly a demand for authorities to take action against Hillary Clinton. But it was more pernicious than that. It was a call for extrajudicial punishment; that implied that the crowd itself should lock her up, as the arbiter of right and wrong, rather than defer to the judiciary. It was a nod to mob rule under his direction.

On 12 August 2017, that message became a little clearer. A 'Unite the Right' rally in Charlottesville, Virginia, featured a number of marchers who proudly described themselves as fascists, brandishing swastika flags and chanting racist slogans, amid other, less explicit far-right groups, euphemistically dubbed the alt-right. The rally turned violent, as demonstrators were met with anti-fascist counter-protesters. A white supremacist rammed his car into a crowd of people, killing one and injuring a further 35. Trump's response was to say that there were 'very fine people on both sides' and also a 'display of hatred, bigotry, and violence on many sides'. In suggesting a moral equivalence, he was legitimising street violence.

Trump's comments cannot be understood in isolation. They constitute a pattern of behaviour, which provokes a set of expected responses. In 2020, during a presidential debate with Biden, he was asked to condemn violence by white supremacists and militia groups. He asked which groups in particular, and Biden referenced the Proud Boys, a far-right street-fighting organisation. Trump responded by saying: 'Proud Boys, stand back and stand by.' He then said: 'But I'll tell you what, somebody's got to do something about Antifa and the left, because this is not a right-wing problem, this is a left-wing [problem].'

Like many of the garbled statements that emerged from Trump's half-broken brain, this could be interpreted in any number of ways. But the response of the Proud Boys themselves was far more revealing. They took it as a moment of recognition and of command. T-shirts were made with the phrase: 'Proud Boys: Standing By'. On social media site Parler, Proud Boys national chair Enrique Tarrio wrote: 'I will stand down sir!!! Standing by sir. So Proud of my guys right now.'

The fact that Trump spoke so confusingly offered deniability. Just like Hitler with his Brownshirts, he never outright told far-right thugs to commit violence. But the implicit message was received clearly by those who had been trained to decode it.

Historians and commentators who had resisted attempts to label Trump a fascist were forced to reconsider on 6 January 2021, when he addressed supporters in Washington DC ahead of the certification of Biden's election win. He had already spent two months denying the validity of the result and pressuring state and federal officials to overturn it – an unprecedented rejection of the core democratic principle of the peaceful transfer of power. 'We will stop the steal,' he said. Then: 'We will never give up. We will never concede. It doesn't happen.' And finally: 'If you don't fight like hell you're not going to have a country anymore.' Moments after the address finished, a mob attacked the US Capitol in an unsuccessful attempt to subvert American democracy. And that was the consequence of the dynamic Trump had developed, in which he spoke in general terms – never openly calling for violence – on the understanding that his followers would know what to do.

It was then that the balance of judgement on Trump's relationship to fascism fundamentally altered. He detached himself from the global populist movement. For all their flaws, figures like Le Pen in France and Geert Wilders in the Netherlands had not questioned election results, let alone tried to overthrow them. Trump alone had resolved to overthrow American democracy through legal chicanery, intimidation and mob violence.

Whether he was aware of it or not, he was forsaking the deal with democracy that far-right parties had made since 1945. It is difficult to consider anyone a fascist if they allow free and fair elections and then accept the result. But the moment this test is failed, the question becomes a live one.

This should have been the moment when Trump's enablers stepped back from the brink and denounced once and for all his violent, anti-democratic politics. But that did not happen, partly because they were terrified of his supporters. Some Republican senators later revealed they had failed to vote for Trump's impeachment for 'incitement of insurrection' out of fear for their safety. Judges and poll workers publicly targeted by Trump also received death threats. Unpunished, he entered the 2024 presidential campaign as the clear frontrunner for the Republican nomination and swept the primaries.

Former Trump appointees at the Heritage Foundation think-tank drew up Project 2025, a radical right-wing programme that would, among other things, give Trump direct control over the federal bureaucracy, roll back civil liberties, promote Christian nationalism and place illegal immigrants in internment camps prior to deportation. Meanwhile, the conservative-dominated Supreme Court ruled that presidents were immune from prosecution for official acts, removing legal guardrails from a second Trump administration.

Opinion polls indicated that tens of millions of Americans heard his increasingly fascist rhetoric and decided that they wanted him back in the White House. One of the core lessons of fascist history went unlearned.

★

On 24 February 2022, Vladimir Putin escalated the war that had been simmering in Ukraine since 2014 into an outright military invasion. It was an event that wove the disparate threads of twenty-first-century populism into a far more coherent pattern.

Putin insisted that his mission was to 'denazify' Ukraine. Needless to say, this statement had no validity whatsoever. It was simply part of the Stalinist tradition of using 'fascist' to condemn enemies, regardless of their political identity. In reality, it was his own nationalist war of unprovoked aggression, driven by genocidal rhetoric, that invited comparisons to 1930s fascism.

After the invasion, Timothy Snyder published an essay called 'We Should Say It. Russia Is Fascist'. 'Today's Russia meets most of the criteria that scholars tend to apply,' he wrote. 'It has a cult around a single leader . . . It has a cult of the dead, organised around World War II. It has a myth of a past golden age of imperial greatness, to be restored by a war of healing violence . . . A time traveller from the 1930s would have no difficulty identifying the Putin regime as fascist.'

Other scholars countered that Putin had not established a revolutionary new kind of regime, and that it was really just 'an aggressive, imperialist, authoritarian state with a ruling junta'. Still, it bears most of the hallmarks of fascism. Putin guts democracy, suppresses dissent, persecutes opponents and minority groups, produces the most flagrant propaganda, controls every arm of the state, wages wars of territorial expansion, seeks power for life, and promotes a myth of national rebirth through power and violence, embodied by himself.

Yet at the same time, due to Russia's wartime history, he must claim to be an anti-fascist. This doublespeak explains his peculiar appeal to populists at both ends of the political spectrum. His supporters on the far left, attracted by his demonisation of the West and their lingering Cold War attachment to Russia, endorse his rhetoric about 'denazifying' Ukraine. Those on the far right, who admire him as an illiberal strongman, are not offended by his anti-fascism because they know he is not sincere, and because they too tar their enemies on the left and centre with the fascist brush. Nobody has been as adept as Putin at weaponising the definitional confusion around fascism.

The war in Ukraine served as a kind of litmus test for populist and authoritarian leaders around the world. The more moderate and pragmatic, such as Meloni, condemned what Putin had done and offered military aid to Ukraine. Orbán, on the other hand, worked to undermine European solidarity with Ukraine from inside the EU. As a presidential candidate, Trump pressured Republican lawmakers to kill off US military and financial support.

Depressing though it may be to contemplate, Putin is arguably the defining figure of the early twenty-first century. He has created the closest modern analogies to the Europe of the early twentieth century. Of all the despots since 1945, it is Putin who Hitler and Mussolini would have most quickly recognised as one of their own.

EPILOGUE
The Story of Fascism

The story of fascism is a journey taken in darkness, where nothing can be seen clearly and events resist clarification. From the very beginning, it was ill-defined. Mussolini pieced together ideas out of immediate political convenience rather than any kind of coherent intellectual viewpoint. Even for Hitler, fascism represented a broiling collection of instincts and paranoias more than an ideological programme. In the second half of the twentieth century, various tyrants and authoritarians emerged who seemed to stand for something similarly despicable but who did not satisfy all the conditions that had been established in Italy and Germany. And now, in the early twenty-first century, we seem surrounded by figures who can't reliably be called fascists but who trade in similar feelings and inspire similar anxieties in their opponents. That makes us want to call them fascists – to shake people by the collar and tell them that we've played this game before and it did not end well. But it deprives us of the confidence to do so, because we're never quite sure if we're using the word correctly, or if deploying it will make us look like hysterics.

Where does all this leave us? What actually *is* fascism? When can we use the word with validity today? What, ultimately, is the meaning of this horrifying story?

There are no easy answers here. There is no flawless, objective test for fascism. This is not due to any weakness in scholarly analysis, but to the weakness of fascism itself. We can define socialism very easily, as the collective ownership of the means of production. We can define liberalism as the belief in the freedom of the individual. That is because these are both meaningful political traditions with a huge body of intellectual contributions. We struggle to define fascism because it is not a meaningful political tradition and it has few, if any, intellectual contributions.

Some historians believe that the word fascism shouldn't be used at all unless it is describing a movement that closely replicates that of the Italian or German fascists in the early twentieth century. But as we've seen, fascism is difficult to define even in this period, because it was such a heady, base-less, doctrine-free phenomenon. We can, however, make a few confident claims about the 1919–45 version of fascism. It arose in a post-war world of economic, political and spiritual crisis, with democracies flailing and leftist revolutionaries seemingly on the rise. It excited its followers and gave their lives meaning. They saw themselves as the shock troops of the future, granted the opportunity to remake their nations.

Fascism established a set of ideas and a new way of organising the state, but its most important characteristic might be its enemies. You could define it by what it hated: communism, liberalism, pluralism, materialism, democracy and all manner of foes within and without. These enemies were irredeemably evil and all-powerful. To the fascist, all opposition was illegitimate and unpatriotic, thus justifying the use of force in defence of the national spirit.

Fascist movements were conservative in some ways, such

as the enforcement of gender norms, and revolutionary in others, such as the annihilation of private life. They proposed from the very start that violence is beautiful, in and of itself, rather than an ugly necessity. They sought to subsume the individual into the identity of the party, nation or race (which they often believed were the same thing), visually reinforcing this mass conformity with uniforms and parades. Their chosen group was always under attack, eaten away by its foes and its own loss of purpose, and had to be aggressively purified in order to rise again.

Fascism could not be understood purely in terms of political systems. There was a religious element too. It moved simultaneously backwards and forwards. Like conservatism, it exploited nostalgia for a mythic past of strength, certainty and rock-solid hierarchies. But it also promised to revive those values in a thrilling future of dynamic young men in fast machines. This sense of history figured in many ancient religions: the world was stuck in a decayed present, between a glorious past and a glorious future. The transition would be necessarily violent. Fascism therefore became an apocalyptic 'civic religion' that pledged to use blood to sluice the road to a utopia that it never precisely defined.

In practice, fascism was fractious, incoherent and volatile, but it sold itself on simplicity. It promised to tidy up the mess of life: not just politics and economics but race, gender, art, history and sex. It sliced the world in two: the clean and the unclean, the righteous and the wicked, us and them. The popular idea that Hitler and Mussolini crept up slowly, concealing their true intentions until it was too late, is a myth. They made their intentions clear; it's just that many people who could have stopped them either did not believe them or were convinced they could control them.

If fascism occurred when certain ideas met certain conditions in certain countries at certain times, then it is fair to say that a modern version of fascism would not meet all of the same criteria. It would not require uniformed militias, fear of a communist revolution, the aftermath of a world war or a global depression. It might well make the pretence of operating within a democratic system, like Vladimir Putin's 'managed democracy'. Elections could still happen, but they wouldn't change anything. So if the search for modern fascism is the search for a Fourth Reich, we will never find it. To subscribe to an entirely historical definition is effectively to say that the word can never be used after 1945.

Fascism signifies horror. The word has come to encapsulate the possibilities of evil at the furthest reaches of right-wing thought. It is therefore a profoundly useful word, one that can function as an emergency warning in dire political circumstances. The fact that it has been devalued through overuse does not delegitimise its application altogether.

Even so, it cannot simply be a catch-all injunction, without any firm connection to what fascist parties actually did or what they thought. Without something to ground it in, we run the danger of falling into the Stalinist trick of using the term simply to denote 'the enemy'.

So if we do want to retain the word as a wake-up call, how do we evaluate when it is right to use it? There are two traditional approaches, both of them suboptimal. The first is to put forward a phrase that sums up the essence of fascism, and the second is to provide a checklist of the qualities it needs to possess.

British scholar Roger Griffin attempted the first by

describing fascism's 'mythic core' as 'a palingenetic form of populist ultranationalism' – palingenesis meaning national rebirth. In *How Fascism Works*, Jason Stanley suggested 'ultra-nationalism of some variety . . . with the nation represented in the person of an authoritarian leader who speaks on its behalf'. But any one-line description of the phenomenon is bound to fall short. Does the concept of national rebirth really deserve the centrality that Griffin gives it? Does Stanley's definition really only apply to fascism?

Checklists, like Umberto Eco's 14-point assessment of 'Ur-Fascism', therefore seem more compelling. Most scholars of fascism come up with something along these lines: the absolute primacy of the group over other groups; a narrative of victimhood, usually overlaid with a conspiracy theory about the elite forces that have undermined the group; a myth of national renewal; a belief that might is right; a love of violence; a hatred of one's opponents and disdain for compromise; a visceral contempt for socialism and to a lesser extent liberalism; a wary but pragmatic relationship with capitalism; total obedience to the leader; the rejection of democracy; the complete submission of the individual to the group identity.

With such a list in hand, you can then start assessing individual populists to see how many marks they get. Primacy of the group? Check. Victimhood narrative? Check. The demonisation of opponents? Check.

But how many characteristics would someone need to possess before we can brand them a fascist? Is it 60 per cent? One hundred? And which elements should carry the most weight? There is no answer to this question. There is no authority to adjudicate it. This is not mathematics. Whether someone has satisfied the requirements is up to each of us as individuals, based on the historical facts and the level of alarm we think is warranted.

Unfortunately, most of us are very bad at making those judgements. We're prone to either writing off anyone who uses the word 'fascist' as a hysteric, or deploying it too hastily. And the more some people do the latter, the more other people revert to the former, turning fascism into a word that says more about the person speaking it than it does about the objective world. It leaves us in a terrible muddle.

One solution is semantic: terms that allude to someone or something having fascist elements without necessarily satisfying the full definition. President Biden referred to Trump's philosophy as 'semi-fascism', a term also used by the historian Stanley Payne. There are many other variants: proto-fascism, quasi-fascism or borderline fascism. And there is the term 'fascistic', to describe a particular element of a populist movement.

These phrases can seem slightly cowardly and evasive, but they're actually very helpful. They provide options. They let you point to worrying elements of a movement or party without having to go all the way. They add nuance while retaining the capacity for historical comparison and political warning.

But the real meaning of the story we have told here is not ultimately about language. It is not even intellectual. It is moral.

What unites these disparate post-1945 figures we have discussed? What is the thread that passes through the glamour-tyranny of Perón, the dead-eyed brutality of Putin, the reality-TV hucksterism of Trump? They come from different traditions, in different countries, at different times, and lead to different outcomes. But they share a common emotional heritage with fascism: the same assumptions and urges, the same narrative framework, the same psychological impulses. They are broken mirrors, showing a fractured and contorted version of the same face.

If anything, fascism is a mood. It is an instinct – a twitch in the brain that urges people to punch instead of think, to hate instead of debate. It offers a darkly attractive binary opposition in which our own group is entirely virtuous and mistreated while everyone else is duplicitous and depraved. It is the urge to pretend that the world is simple and that the terrible things that happen are the result of a wicked conspiracy. It is the fear of weakness and the thrill of asserting our dominance through strength. It is the temptation to submit ourselves to the group, to forsake thought, to find belonging in the mass. It is the frustration that emerges during moments of crisis, when traditional parties struggle to provide answers to our problems and we find ourselves wishing for a strongman to sweep the complexity away. The French philosopher Michel Foucault warned against 'the fascism in us all, in our heads and in our everyday behaviour, the fascism that causes us to love power, to desire the very thing that dominates and exploits us'.

This is the lesson to take from the story of fascism. It is not about how to define it. It is about how we protect ourselves from the ideas that gave rise to it. As Richard J. Evans wrote at the end of his three-volume history of Nazism: 'The Third Reich raises in the most acute form the possibilities and consequences of the human hatred and destructiveness that exists, even if only in a small way, within all of us. It demonstrates with terrible clarity the ultimate potential consequences of racism, militarism and authoritarianism. It shows what can happen if some people are treated as less human than others.'

The best response to this story is a personal commitment to cultivate in ourselves the values that stand opposed to the ideas that formed fascism. That means nurturing individual freedom, seeking consensus and moderation instead of absolute victory, protecting minorities, committing ourselves to rational, independent thought, spurning conformity, refusing to worship leaders, and recognising the equal value of all people, no matter their background or ethnicity. Most of all, it means rejecting the politics of Us versus Them. It is, in short, to be an anti-fascist.

Acknowledgements

Our thanks to the whole team at Orion, who worked so diligently to make these books happen. They are: Lindsay Terrell, Lily McIlwain, Jo Whitford, Jane Selley, Aoife Datta, and Dan Jackson, who designed the beautiful retro covers and orchestrated the design scheme across the line. Most of all, thank you to Jenny Lord, who believed in this project pretty much from the second we put out our first episode and helped carry us every step of the way. Without her, these books would not exist.

Thanks to the production team at Podmasters, who really are responsible for *Origin Story* as it stands today. They didn't just give us the equipment. They forced us to think hard about what we wanted to do and refine the idea until it became a viable editorial proposition. In particular, thank you to Andrew Harrison, Martin Bojtos, Simon Williams, Anne-Marie Luff, Jade Bailey, Jim Parrett, Mischa Welsh, Kieron Leslie, Jill Pearson and Jessica Harpin.

Most of all, thank you to our listeners. Nothing about *Origin Story* made sense when we conceived of it. It would entail countless hours of work for each episode and break away from the current affairs ecosystem, in which we had an inbuilt audience, to try something completely different. There was a danger that it would be too light-hearted for the serious-minded people and too serious for the light-hearted people. But we knew that we wanted something unusual and were delighted to find out that other people did too. Thanks to each and every one of you, but thanks especially to the Patreons, whose kind financial support makes the podcast possible – and these books as well.

Ian

Thanks to my agent, Lisa Moylett, who always has my back. Thanks to my parents, whose love and support is the precondition of anything I've managed to accomplish. Thanks to the London Clan of Shazia and Farrah and the Old School Gang of Souster, Swinden and Westy. Thanks most of all to Menissa, without whom nothing is possible or even worth considering. Finally, thank you to Richard Evans, whose trilogy on the Third Reich greatly informed the book you're holding in your hands right now.

Dorian

Thanks to Lucy, Eleanor and Luke for their love, support and essential good vibes while I was navigating a dark subject. Thanks to Antony Topping, my stalwart agent. Thanks to the late Sidney Weiland, for teaching me to ask the right questions and not settle for simple answers. And existential gratitude to my grandparents Maria and Beno for surviving fascism against the odds.

Bibliography

General history

Madeleine Albright, *Fascism: A Warning* (William Collins, 2019)

Hannah Arendt, *The Origins of Totalitarianism* (Penguin Classics, 2017; first published 1951)

Frank Dikötter, *Dictators: The Cult of Personality in the Twentieth Century* (Bloomsbury, 2020)

Ian Dunt, *How to Be a Liberal: The Story of Freedom and the Fight for its Survival* (Canbury, 2020)

Roger Eatwell, *Fascism: A History* (Chatto & Windus, 1995)

Umberto Eco, 'Ur-Fascism' (1995), in *How to Spot a Fascist*, translated by Richard Dixon and Alastair McEwen (Harvill Secker, 2020)

Stephen Graham, *The Faces of Fascism: Mussolini, Hitler & Franco: Their Paths to Power* (BLKDOG, 2023)

Roger Griffin, *The Nature of Fascism* (Routledge, 1993)

Eric Hobsbawm, *The Age of Extremes: The Short Twentieth Century, 1914–1991* (Penguin, 1994)

Michael Mann, *Fascists* (Cambridge University Press, 2004)

Paul Mason, *How to Stop Fascism* (Allen Lane, 2021)

Michael S. Neiberg, *Warfare and Society in Europe: 1898 to the Present* (Routledge, 2004)

Ernst Nolte, *Three Faces of Fascism*, translated by Leila Vennewitz (Holt, Rinehart and Winston, 1965)

Kevin Passmore, *Fascism: A Very Short Introduction* (Oxford University Press, 2014)

Robert O. Paxton, *The Anatomy of Fascism* (Penguin, 2005)

Stanley G. Payne, *A History of Fascism 1914–1945* (University of Wisconsin Press, 1995)

Jason Stanley, *How Fascism Works: The Politics of Us and Them* (Random House, 2018)

Lyndsey Stonebridge, *We Are Free to Change the World: Hannah Arendt's Lessons in Love and Disobedience* (Jonathan Cape, 2024)

A. J. P. Taylor, *The Origins of the Second World War* (Penguin, 1964)

Alberto Toscano, *Late Fascism: Race, Capitalism and the Politics of Crisis* (Verso, 2023)

Italian fascism

Italo Calvino, 'Il Duce's Portraits', *New Yorker*, 29 December 2002

Count Galeazzo Ciano, *The Ciano Diaries 1939–1943*, edited by Hugh Gibson (Simon Publications, 2001)

Richard Collier, *Duce! A Biography of Benito Mussolini* (Viking Press, 1971)

Christopher Duggan, *Fascist Voices: An Intimate History of Mussolini's Italy* (Oxford University Press, 2013)

Nicholas Farrell, *Mussolini: A New Life* (Sharpe Books, 2018)

Giuseppe Finaldi, *Mussolini and Italian Fascism* (Pearson, 2008)

John Foot, *Blood and Power: The Rise and Fall of Italian Fascism* (Bloomsbury, 2023)

Christopher Hibbert, *Il Duce: The Life of Benito Mussolini* (Little, Brown and Company, 1962)

Lucy Hughes-Hallett, *The Pike: Gabriele D'Annunzio, Poet,*

Seducer and Preacher of War (Fourth Estate, 2013)

Gregor A. James, *Young Mussolini and the Intellectual Origins of Fascism* (University of California Press, 1979)

Emil Ludwig, *Talks with Mussolini*, translated by Eden and Cedar Paul (Little, Brown, 1933)

Denis Mack Smith, *Mussolini* (Phoenix Giants, 1994)

Gaudens Megaro, *Mussolini in the Making* (Houghton Mifflin, 1938)

Ray Moseley, *Mussolini: The Last 600 Days of Il Duce* (Taylor Trade Publishing, 2004)

Benito Mussolini, *The Doctrine of Fascism* (Howard Fertig, 2006)

Peter Neville, *Mussolini* (Routledge, 2004)

Giorgio Pini, *The Official Life of Benito Mussolini*, translated by Luigi Villari (Hutchinson & Co., 1939)

German fascism

Anthony Beevor, *The Second World War* (Weidenfeld & Nicolson, 2012)

Wilhelm Deist and E. J. Feuchtwanger, 'The Military Collapse of the German Empire: The Reality Behind the Stab-in-the-Back Myth', *War in History*, Vol. 3, No. 2 (April 1996)

Max Domarus, *The Complete Hitler: Speeches and Proclamations 1932–1945* (Bolchazy-Carducci Publishers, 1990)

Richard J. Evans, *The Coming of the Third Reich* (Penguin, 2004)

——, *The Third Reich in Power* (Penguin, 2006)

——, *The Third Reich at War* (Penguin, 2009)

Henry Friedlander, *The Origins of Nazi Genocide: From Euthanasia to the Final Solution* (University of North Carolina Press, 1997)

BIBLIOGRAPHY

Robert Gellately, *Backing Hitler: Consent and Coercion in Nazi Germany* (Oxford University Press, 2013)

Adolf Hitler, *Mein Kampf*, translated by James Murphy (Hurst and Blackett, 1942)

Rudolf Höss, *Commandant of Auschwitz: The Autobiography of Rudolf Höss* (World Publishing Company, 1951)

Victor Klemperer, *I Shall Bear Witness: The Diaries of Victor Klemperer, 1933–41*, translated by Martin Chalmers (BCA, 1998)

——, *To the Bitter End: The Diaries of Victor Klemperer, 1942–1945*, translated by Martin Chalmers (BCA, 1999)

——, *The Lesser Evil: The Diaries of Victor Klemperer, 1945–1959*, translated by Martin Chalmers (BCA, 2003)

H. R. Knickerbocker, *Is Tomorrow Hitler's? 200 Questions on the Battle of Mankind* (Reynal & Hitchcock, 1941)

Guido Knopp, *Hitler's Henchmen* (Sutton, 2000)

Melita Maschmann, *Account Rendered: A Dossier on My Former Self*, translated by Geoffrey Strachan (Plunkett Lake Press, April 2013)

Peter H. Merkl, *Political Violence Under the Swastika: 581 Early Nazis* (Princeton University Press, 1975)

Emmanuel Ringelblum, *Notes from the Warsaw Ghetto: The Journal of Emmanuel Ringelblum*, edited and translated by Jacob Sloan (Schocken Books, 1974)

Alex Scobie, *Hitler's State Architecture: The Impact of Classical Antiquity* (Philadelphia, 1990)

William L. Shirer, *Berlin Diary: The Journal of a Foreign Correspondent, 1934–1941* (Blackstone, 2011)

Timothy Snyder, *Bloodlands: Europe Between Hitler and Stalin* (Vintage, 2015)

Albert Speer, *Inside the Third Reich: Memoirs*, translated by Richard and Clara Winston (Macmillan, 1970)

William II, *My Memoirs 1878–1918* (Cassell and Company, 1922)

International fascism

Edwin Black, *War Against the Weak: Eugenics and America's Campaign to Create a Master Race* (Four Walls Eight Windows, 2003)

Sarah Churchwell, *Behold, America: A History of America First and the American Dream* (Bloomsbury, 2019)

Stephen Dorril, *Blackshirt: Sir Oswald Mosley and British Fascism* (Penguin, 2007)

Julie V. Gottlieb, *Feminine Fascism: Women in Britain's Fascist Movement 1923–1945* (I. B. Tauris, 2000)

Gabrielle Ashford Hodges, *Franco: A Concise Biography* (Weidenfeld & Nicolson, 2000)

Paul Preston, *The Spanish Civil War: Reaction, Revolution and Revenge* (W. W. Norton & Co., 2007)

Modern fascism

Attila Antal, *The Rise of Hungarian Populism: State Autocracy and the Orbán Regime* (Emerald Publishing, 2019)

Zygmunt Bauman, *Modernity and the Holocaust* (Polity, 1991)

Zack Beauchamp, 'It Happened There: How Democracy Died in Hungary', *Vox*, 13 September 2018

Federico Finchelstein, *From Fascism to Populism in History* (University of California Press, 2019)

Giorgio Ghiglione, 'Why Giorgia Meloni Won't Distance Herself from Italy's Fascist Past', *Foreign Policy*, 6 February 2023

Adam Gopnik, 'Calling Trump the F-Word', *New Yorker*, 12 September 2022

Robert Kagan, 'This Is How Fascism Comes to America', Brookings Institution, 22 May 2016

Peter Kreko, 'Anti-Muslim sentiments and disinformation in Hungary', Center for European Policy Analysis

Judd Legum, 'A Poisonous Campaign', Popular Information, 2 January 2024

Chris Lehmann, 'The "Is Donald Trump a Fascist?" Debate Has Been Ended – by Donald Trump', *The Nation*, 14 November 2023

Paul Lendvai, *Orbán: Europe's New Strongman* (Hurst, 2019)

Dylan Matthews, 'Is Trump a Fascist? 8 Experts Weigh In', *Vox*, 23 October 2020

Cas Mudde, *The Far Right Today* (Polity, 2019)

Kinga Rajzak, 'How Hungary's media created the "Muslim bogeyman"', *Al Jazeera Journalism Review*, 28 December 2022

Luigi Scazzieri, 'Can Meloni's balancing act continue?', Centre for European Reform, 21 August 2023

Adam Serwer, 'The Cruelty Is the Point', *The Atlantic*, 3 October 2018

Timothy Snyder, *The Road to Unfreedom: Russia, Europe, America* (The Bodley Head, 2018)

Timothy Snyder, 'We Should Say It. Russia Is Fascist', *New York Times*, 18 May 2022

Other sources

Paul Berman, *Terror and Liberalism* (W. W. Norton & Co., 2003)

Bertolt Brecht, *Galileo*, edited by Eric Bentley (Grove Press, 1966)

Albert Camus, *The Plague*, translated by Stuart Gilbert

(Penguin, 1960; first published 1947)

Guy Debord, *The Society of the Spectacle*, translated by Donald Nicholson-Smith (Zone, 1994; first published 1967)

Gustave Le Bon, *The Crowd: A Study of the Popular Mind* (T. Fisher Unwin, 1909; first published 1896)

Filippo Tommaso Marinetti, *The Futurist Manifesto* (1909)

John Morrow, *History of Political Thought* (Macmillan, 1998)

George Orwell, *Complete Works X: A Kind of Compulsion 1903–36* (Secker & Warburg, 2000)

George Orwell, *Complete Works XII: A Patriot After All 1940–1941* (Secker & Warburg, 2000)

George Orwell, *Complete Works XVI: I Have Tried to Tell the Truth 1943–1944* (Secker & Warburg, 2001)

Georges Sorel, *Reflections on Violence*, translated by T. E. Hulme and J. Roth (Collier, 1961)

Ignazio Silone, *The School for Dictators*, translated by Gwenda David and Eric Mosbacher (Jonathan Cape, 1939)

Dorothy Thompson, 'Who Goes Nazi?', *Harper's Magazine*, August 1941

Index

INDEX

INDEX

INDEX

INDEX

INDEX

INDEX

INDEX